LSAT
LOGIC GAMES

ULTIMATE SETUPS
GUIDE

POWERSCORE®
TEST PREPARATION

PowerScore Publishing
37V New Orleans Road
Hilton Head Island, SC 29928

Author: David M. Killoran

Manufactured in Canada
November 2007

ISBN: 978-1-60530-358-1

CONTENTS

CHAPTER ONE: INTRODUCTION

CHAPTER TWO: FEBRUARY 1995 LSAT GAMES

CHAPTER THREE: JUNE 1995 LSAT GAMES

CHAPTER FOUR: SEPTEMBER 1995 LSAT GAMES

CHAPTER FIVE: DECEMBER 1995 LSAT GAMES

CHAPTER SIX: JUNE 1996 LSAT GAMES

CHAPTER SEVEN: OCTOBER 1996 LSAT GAMES

CHAPTER EIGHT: DECEMBER 1996 LSAT GAMES

CHAPTER NINE: FEBRUARY 1997 LSAT GAMES

CHAPTER TEN: JUNE 1997 LSAT GAMES

CHAPTER ELEVEN: OCTOBER 1997 LSAT GAMES

CHAPTER TWELVE: DECEMBER 1997 LSAT GAMES

CHAPTER THIRTEEN: JUNE 1998 LSAT GAMES

CHAPTER FOURTEEN: SEPTEMBER 1998 LSAT GAMES

CHAPTER FIFTEEN: DECEMBER 1998 LSAT GAMES

CHAPTER SIXTEEN: JUNE 1999 LSAT GAMES

CHAPTER SEVENTEEN: OCTOBER 1999 LSAT GAMES

CHAPTER EIGHTEEN: DECEMBER 1999 LSAT GAMES

CHAPTER NINETEEN: JUNE 2000 LSAT GAMES

CHAPTER TWENTY: OCTOBER 2000 LSAT GAMES

CHAPTER TWENTY ONE: DECEMBER 2000 LSAT GAMES

CHAPTER TWENTY TWO: JUNE 2001 LSAT GAMES

Chapter Twenty Three: October 2001 LSAT Games

Chapter Twenty Four: December 2001 LSAT Games

Chapter Twenty Five: June 2002 LSAT Games

Chapter Twenty Six: October 2002 LSAT Games

Chapter Twenty Seven: December 2002 LSAT Games

Endnotes

About PowerScore

PowerScore is one of the nation's fastest growing test preparation companies. Headquartered on Hilton Head Island in South Carolina, PowerScore offers LSAT, GMAT, GRE, and SAT preparation classes in over 100 locations in the U.S. and abroad. For more information, please visit our website at www.powerscore.com.

CHAPTER ONE: INTRODUCTION

Introduction

Welcome to the *PowerScore LSAT Logic Games Ultimate Setups Guide*. The purpose of this book is to provide you with complete setups for each game in the Analytical Reasoning section of the Law School Admission Test (LSAT), and this book contains setups for every numbered LSAT PrepTest game released between February 1995 to December 2002.

The *Ultimate Setups Guide* is intended to be a companion book to the *PowerScore LSAT Logic Games Bible*. Many of the references in this book, including the diagramming methodology and approach we use, are explained in detail in the *Logic Games Bible*, and a working knowledge of those techniques will increase the value you derive from the *Ultimate Setups Guide*. If you do not currently own a copy of the *PowerScore LSAT Logic Games Bible*, we strongly recommend that you purchase one immediately. If you already own a copy of the *Bible*, we recommend that you complete that book prior to using this book.

Each chapter of this book contains setups and notes for each of the four Logic Games that appears on each released LSAT. This book does *not* contain reproductions of the games themselves. This is because not all games can currently be licensed. For example, LSATs such as the February 2002 LSAT cannot yet be licensed, and therefore they cannot be reproduced. However, many of the tests can be purchased directly from PowerScore or Law Services. In order to prepare as thoroughly as possible, we strongly recommend that you purchase as many tests as possible.

The LSATs containing the Logic Games covered in this book can be purchased through our website at powerscore.com.

Because new LSATs appear every several months, and access to accurate and up-to-date information is critical, we have devoted a section of our website to *Ultimate Setups Guide* students. This free online resource area offers supplements to the book material, provides updates, lists every LSAT PrepTest and the corresponding Law Services publication signifier, and classifies every LSAT Logic Game. There is also an official book evaluation form that we strongly encourage you to use. The exclusive *LSAT Logic Games Ultimate Setups Guide* online area can be accessed at:

www.powerscore.com/lgsetups

If we can assist you in your LSAT preparation in any way, or if you have any questions or comments, please do not hesitate to contact us via email at lgsetups@powerscore.com. Additional contact information is provided at the end of this book. We look forward to hearing from you!

A Brief Overview of the LSAT

The Law School Admission Test is administered four times a year: in February, June, September/October, and December. This standardized test is required for admission to any American Bar Association-approved law school. According to Law Services, the producers of the test, the LSAT is designed "to measure skills that are considered essential for success in law school: the reading and comprehension of complete texts with accuracy and insight; the organization and management of information and the ability to draw reasonable inferences from it; the ability to reason critically; and the analysis and evaluation of the reasoning and argument of others." The LSAT consists of the following five sections:

- •2 Sections of Logical Reasoning (short arguments, 24-26 total questions)
- •1 Section of Reading Comprehension (3 long reading passages, 2 short comparative reading passages, 26-28 total questions)
- •1 Section of Analytical Reasoning (4 logic games, 22-24 total questions)
- •1 Experimental Section of one of the above three section types.

You are given 35 minutes to complete each section. The experimental section is unscored and is not returned to the test taker. A break of 10 to 15 minutes is given between the 3rd and 4th sections.

The five-section test is followed by a 35 minute writing sample.

The Logical Reasoning Section

Each Logical Reasoning Section is composed of approximately 24 to 26 short arguments. Every short argument is followed by a question such as: "Which one of the following weakens the argument?" "Which one of the following parallels the argument?" or "Which one of the following must be true according to the argument?" The key to this section is time management and an understanding of the reasoning types and question types that frequently appear.

Since there are two scored sections of Logical Reasoning on every LSAT, this section accounts for approximately 50% of your score.

The Analytical Reasoning Section

This section, also known as Logic Games, is probably the most difficult for students taking the LSAT for the first time. The section consists of four games or puzzles, each followed by a series of five to eight questions. The questions are designed to test your ability to evaluate a set of relationships and to make inferences about those relationships. To perform well on this section you must understand the major types of games that frequently appear and develop the ability to properly diagram the rules and make inferences.

When you take an actual LSAT, they take your thumbprint at the testing site. This is done in case of test security problems.

At the conclusion of the LSAT, and for six calendar days after the LSAT, you have the option to cancel your score. Unfortunately, there is no way to determine exactly what your score would be before cancelling.

The Reading Comprehension Section

This section is composed of three long reading passages, each approximately 450 words in length, and two shorter comparative reading passages. The passage topics are drawn from a variety of subjects, and each passage is followed by a series of five to eight questions that ask you to determine viewpoints in the passage, analyze organizational traits, evaluate specific sections of the passage, or compare facets of two different passages. The key to this section is to read quickly with understanding and to carefully analyze the passage structure.

The Experimental Section

Each LSAT contains one experimental section, and it does not count towards your score. The experimental can be any of the three section types described above, and the purpose of the section is to test and evaluate questions that will be used on *future* LSATs. By pretesting questions before their use in a scored section, the experimental helps the makers of the test determine the test scale.

The Writing Sample

A 35 minute Writing Sample is given at the conclusion of the LSAT. The Writing Sample is not scored, but a copy is sent to each of the law schools to which you apply.

For many years the Writing Sample was administered before the LSAT.

The format of the Writing Sample is called the Decision Prompt: you are asked to consider two possible courses of action, decide which one is superior, and then write a short essay supporting your choice. Each course of action is described in a short paragraph and you are given two primary criteria to consider in making your decision. Typically the two courses of action each have different strengths and weaknesses, and there is no clearly correct decision.

Do not agonize over the Writing Sample; in law school admissions, the Writing Sample is usually not a determining element for three reasons: the admissions committee is aware that the essay is given after a grueling three hour test and is about a subject you have no personal interest in; they already have a better sample of your writing ability in the personal statement; and the committee has a limited amount of time to evaluate applications.

You must attempt the Writing Sample! If you do not, Law Services reserves the right not to score your test.

The LSAT Scoring Scale

Each administered LSAT contains approximately 101 questions, and each LSAT score is based on the total number of questions a test taker correctly answers, a total known as the raw score. After the raw score is determined, a unique Score Conversion Chart is used for each LSAT to convert the raw score into a scaled LSAT score. Since June 1991, the LSAT has utilized a 120 to 180 scoring scale, with 120 being the lowest possible score and 180 being the highest possible score. Notably, this 120 to 180 scale is just a renumbered version of the 200 to 800 scale most test takers are familiar with from the SAT and GMAT. Just drop the "1" and add a "0" to the 120 and 180.

Although the number of questions per test has remained relatively constant over the last eight years, the overall logical difficulty of each test has varied. This is not surprising since the test is made by humans and there is no precise way to completely predetermine logical difficulty. To account for these variances in test "toughness," the test makers adjust the Scoring Conversion Chart for each LSAT in order to make similar LSAT scores from different tests mean the same thing. For example, the LSAT given in June may be logically more difficult than the LSAT given in December, but by making the June LSAT scale "looser" than the December scale, a 160 on each test would represent the same level of performance. This scale adjustment, known as equating, is extremely important to law school admissions offices around the country. Imagine the difficulties that would be posed by unequated tests: admissions officers would have to not only examine individual LSAT scores, but also take into account which LSAT each score came from. This would present an information nightmare.

The LSAT Percentile Table

It is important not to lose sight of what LSAT scaled scores actually represent. The 120 to 180 test scale contains 61 different possible scores. Each score places a student in a certain relative position compared to other test takers. These relative positions are represented through a percentile that correlates to each score. The percentile indicates where the test taker ranks in the overall pool of test takers. For example, a score of 163 represents the 90th percentile, meaning a student with a score of 163 scored better than 90 percent of the people who have taken the test in the last three years. The percentile is critical since it is a true indicator of your positioning relative to other test takers, and thus law school applicants.

Since the LSAT has 61 possible scores, why didn't the test makers change the scale to 0 to 60? Probably for merciful reasons. How would you tell your friends that you scored a 3 on the LSAT? 123 sounds so much better.

Charting out the entire percentage table yields a rough "bell curve." The number of test takers in the 120s and 170s is very low (only 1.6% of all test takers receive a score in the 170s), and most test takers are bunched in the middle, comprising the "top" of the bell. In fact, approximately 40% of all test takers score between 145 and 155 inclusive, and about 70% of all test takers score between 140 and 160 inclusive.

The median score on the LSAT scale is approximately 151. The median, or middle, score is the score at which approximately 50% of test takers have a lower score and 50% of test takers have a higher score. Typically, to achieve a score of 151, you must answer between 56 and 61 questions correctly from a total of 101 questions. In other words, to achieve a score that is perfectly average, you can miss between 40 and 45 questions. Thus, it is important to remember that you don't have to answer every question correctly in order to receive an excellent LSAT score. There is room for error, and accordingly you should never let any single question occupy an inordinate amount of your time.

There is no penalty for answering incorrectly on the LSAT. Therefore, you should guess on any questions you cannot complete.

The Use of the LSAT

The use of the LSAT in law school admissions is not without controversy. It is largely taken for granted that your LSAT score is one of the most important determinants of the type of school you can attend. At many law schools a multiplier made up of your LSAT score and your undergraduate grade point average is used to help determine the relative standing of applicants, and at some schools a sufficiently high multiplier guarantees your admission.

For all the importance of the LSAT, it is not without flaws. As a standardized test currently given in the paper-and-pencil format, there are a number of skills that the LSAT cannot measure, such as listening skills, note-taking ability, perseverance, etc. Law Services is aware of these limitations and as a matter of course they warn all law schools about overemphasizing LSAT results. Still, since the test ultimately returns a number for each student, it is hard to escape the tendency to rank applicants accordingly. Fortunately, once you get to law school the LSAT is forgotten. For the time being consider the test a temporary hurdle you must leap in order to reach the ultimate goal.

For more information on the LSAT, or to register for the test, contact Law Services at (215) 968-1001 or at their website at www.lsac.org.

As you know, the focus of this book is on the Analytical Reasoning section. Each Analytical Reasoning section contains four games and a total of 22-24 questions. Since you have thirty-five minutes to complete the section, you have an average of eight minutes and forty-five seconds to complete each game. Of course, the amount of time you spend on each game will vary with the difficulty and the number of questions per game. For many students, the time constraint is what makes Logic Games the most difficult section on the LSAT, and as we progress through this book, we will discuss time management techniques as well as timesaving techniques that you can employ within the section.

On average, you have 8 minutes and 45 seconds to complete each game.

Each logic game contains three separate parts: the scenario, the rules, and the questions. The scenario introduces sets of variables—people, places, things, or events—involved in an easy to understand activity such as sitting in seats or singing songs. Here is an example of a game scenario from the September 1998 LSAT:

> A messenger will deliver exactly seven packages—L, M, N, O, P, S, and T—one at a time, not necessarily in that order. The seven deliveries must be made according to the following conditions:

Always write down and keep track of each variable set.

In the above scenario there are two variable sets: the packages L, M, N, O, P, S, and T, and the seven delivery positions, which would be numbered 1 through 7.

The second part of every game is the rules—a set of statements that describe the relationships between the variables. Here are the rules that accompanied the above game scenario:

> P is delivered either first or seventh.
> The messenger delivers N at some time after delivering L.
> The messenger delivers T at some time after delivering M.
> The messenger delivers exactly one package between delivering L and delivering O, whether or not L is delivered before O.
> The messenger delivers exactly one package between delivering M and delivering P, whether or not M is delivered before P.

The third and final part of each logic game is a set of approximately five to eight questions that test your knowledge of the relationships between the variables, the structural features of the game, and the way those relationships and features change as conditions in the game change.

The initial rules apply to every question unless otherwise indicated.

Each of the initial rules in a game applies to each and every question; however, on occasion a question will explicitly suspend one or more rules for the purposes of that question only. These "suspension" questions always occur at the end of the game.

Approaching the Games

As you begin each game you should carefully and completely read through the entire game scenario and all of the rules *before* you begin writing. This initial reading will help you determine the type of game you are facing, as well as what variable sets exist and what relationships govern their actions. This advice will save you time by allowing you to formulate an exact plan of action, and it will save you from diagramming a rule and then re-diagramming if you find a later rule that alters the situation. At this point in the game you must also fix the rules in your memory. Students who fail to identify strongly with the rules inevitably struggle with the questions. It is also important to identify the most powerful rules in a game and to consider how the rules interact with one another. Of course, we will discuss how to do this throughout our analysis. In general, these are the initial steps you must take to efficiently move through each game:

Always read through the entire scenario and each rule before you begin diagramming.

1. Read through and fix the rules in your mind.
2. Diagram the scenario and the rules.
3. Make inferences.
4. Use the rules and inferences to attack the questions.

Setups and Diagramming

Your initial reading of the game will also indicate what setup to use to attack the game. Many students are not aware of the best ways to set up logic games, and waste far too much time during the actual exam wondering what approach to take. Because you must read the rules and set up a diagram quickly and efficiently, the key to succeeding on the Logic Games section is to know the ideal approach to every game type before walking into the exam.

You should use the space at the bottom of each game page to diagram your initial setup. This setup should include:

Make a main diagram at the bottom of the page.

1. A list of the variables and their number. For example: L M N O P S T ^{7}
2. An identification of any randoms in the game (randoms are variables that do not appear in any rules).
3. A diagrammatic representation of the variable sets.
4. A diagrammatic representation of the rules.
5. A list of inferences. Making inferences involves deducing hidden rules or facts from the given relationships between variables. Inferences almost always follow from a combination of the rules or limiting structural factors within the game.

By following the above list and using the scenario and rules from the September 1998 game on the previous page, we can produce the setup on the following page:

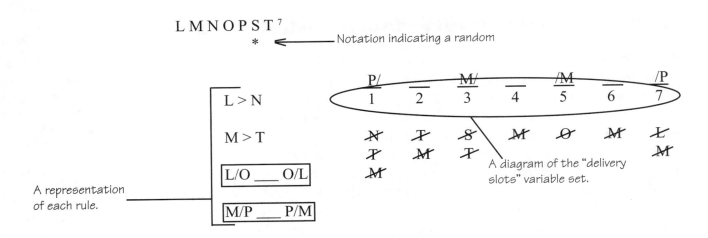

A representation of each rule.

A diagram of the "delivery slots" variable set.

The above setup is linear in nature, and in the next chapter, we will further discuss this type of game, as well as how to create this type of diagram.

After making the initial setup, do not write on your main diagram.

Once you have completed your game setup, you should *not* draw or otherwise write on your main diagram again. As you do each question, use the space *next* to the question to reproduce a miniature diagram with the basic structural features of your main diagram. You should *not* use your main diagram for the work of individual questions. For example, if a question introduces the condition that L sits in the third of seven chairs, draw the seven chair spaces next to the question, place L in the third space, make inferences, and then proceed with the question. Refer to your main setup for the details of the relationship between the variables. There are several important benefits that you receive from working next to the question: First, should you need to return to the question later, your work will be readily available and accessible; second, keeping the individual conditions of each question separate from the main setup reduces the possibility that you will mistake a local condition for a global rule; and third, you will be able to more clearly see which conditions produced which results.

Do the work for each question next to that question.

Do not erase unless you make a mistake.

As you complete each question, it is absolutely essential that you *not* erase your previous work. Each question you complete adds to your repository of game knowledge, and that knowledge can be invaluable when answering other questions. For example, suppose the first question in a game produces a scenario where A is in the first position. Then the second question asks for a complete and accurate listing of the positions A can occupy. Based on the first question, A can clearly be in the first position, and thus you can eliminate any answer in the second question which does not contain the first position as a possibility. Thus, the work you do in *some* questions can be used to help answer other questions. This is true as long as the work you are referencing conforms to the conditions in the question you are currently answering. For example, if the third question in the same game states, "If A is in the third position, which of the following can be true?" then you cannot use the information from the first question to help answer the third question.

The work done on some questions can be used to help solve other questions.

For students who ignore the above recommendations, the results are often quite negative: confusion, disorganization, constant rereading of the rules, and missed questions. Some students say that they save time by using their main diagram for each question. While they may save a short amount of time, the overall costs always outweigh the benefits, particularly since those same students have a tendency to erase during the game. As we proceed with our analysis of the games section, we will revisit this topic from time to time and ultimately prove the efficacy of our recommendations.

The Questions

Once you have completed your diagram and made inferences, you will be ready for the questions. Keep in mind that each question has exactly the same value and that there is no penalty for guessing. Thus, if you cannot complete the section you should guess on the questions that remain. If you cannot complete an individual question, move on and complete the others.

Games questions are either global or local. Global questions ask about information derived only from the initial rules, such as "Who can finish first?" or "Which one of the following must be true?" Use your main diagram to answer global questions. Local questions occur when the question imposes a new condition in addition to the initial rules, such as "If Laura sits in the third chair, which one of the following must be true?" The additional conditions imposed by local questions apply to that question only and do not apply to any of the other questions. It is essential that you focus on the implications of the new conditions. Ask yourself how this condition affects the variables and the existing rules. For local questions, reproduce a mini-setup next to the question, apply the local condition, and proceed. We will discuss how to do this in our games discussion in the next chapter.

> Local questions almost always require you to produce a "mini-setup" next to the question.

Within the global/local designation all questions ultimately ask for one of four things: what must be true, what is not necessarily true, what could be true, and what cannot be true. All questions are a variation of one of these four basic ideas. At all times, you must be aware of the exact nature of the question you are being asked, especially when "except" questions appear. If you find that you are missing questions because you miss words such as "false" or "except" when reading, then take a moment at the beginning of the game to circle the key words in each question, words such as "must," "could," etc.

> If you frequently misread games questions, circle the key part of each question before you begin the game. You will not forget about a word like "except" if you have it underlined!

The key to quickly answering questions is to identify with the rules and inferences in a game. This involves both properly diagramming the rules and simple memorization. If you often find yourself rereading the rules during a game, you are failing to identify with the rules. And do not forget to constantly apply your inferences to each question!

The key to optimal performance on Logic Games is to be focused and organized. This involves a number of factors:

1. Play to your strengths and away from your weaknesses

You are not required to do the games in the order presented on the test, and you should not expect that the test makers will present the games in the best order for you. Students who expect to have difficulty on the games section should attack the games in order of their personal preferences and strengths and weaknesses.

2. Create a strong setup for the game

The key to powerful games performance is often to create a good setup. At least 80% of the games on the LSAT are "setup games" wherein the quality of your setup dictates whether or not you are successful in answering the questions.

3. Look to make inferences

There are always inferences in a game, and the test makers expect you to make at least a few of them. Always check the rules and your setup with an eye towards finding inferences.

4. Be smart during the game

If necessary, skip over time consuming questions and return to them later. Remember that it is sometimes advisable to do the questions out of order. For example, if the first question in a game asks you for a complete and accurate list of the positions "C" could occupy, because of time considerations it would be advisable to skip that question and complete the remaining questions. Then you could return to the first question and use the knowledge you gained from the other questions to quickly and easily answer the first question.

5. Do not be intimidated by size

A lengthy game scenario and a large number of initial rules do not necessarily equal greater difficulty. Some of the longest games are easy because they contain so many restrictions and limitations.

6. Keep an awareness of time

As stated previously, you have approximately eight minutes and forty-five seconds to complete each game and bubble in your answers. Use a timer during the LSAT so you always know how much time remains, and do not let one game or question consume so much time that you suffer later on.

7. Maintain a positive attitude and concentrate

Above all, you must attack each game with a positive and energetic attitude. The games themselves are often challenging yet fun, and students who actively involve themselves in the games generally perform better overall.

If you do all four games, you have 8 minutes and 45 seconds to complete each game, inclusive of answer transferring. If you do only three games, you have 11 minutes and 40 seconds to complete each game. If you do just two games, you have 17 minutes and 30 seconds to complete each game.

Memorize these points! They are basic principles you must know in order to perform powerfully.

You can do the games out of order and according to your strengths and weaknesses.

There are three parts to every Logic Game: the scenario, the rules, and the questions.

Always read the scenario and rules once through before you begin diagramming.

Fix the rules in your mind.

Make a main diagram for each game. Include the following:
    List the variables and their exact total number
    Identify Randoms
    Diagram the variable sets
    Diagram the rules
    Make inferences
    Identify the powerful rules and variables

Write neatly.

You can do the questions out of order if it saves time or is more efficient.

For local questions, do your work next to the question.

Always look to use your inferences when answering questions.

Do not erase unless you have made a mistake.

Do not forget that work from one question might be useful on other questions.

Maintain a positive attitude, concentrate, and try to enjoy yourself.

Game Setup Usage Notes

The following pages contain game setups organized by chapter. Each chapter contains the setups for the four games from a single LSAT, and the chapters are presented in order according to the date the test was given.

The chapters do not have traditional "chapter divider" headings. Instead, at the top of each page is a game indicator, for example, "June 1995 Game #1: Questions 1-6." At the bottom of each right-hand page is a reference to the month and year of the LSAT games in the chapter, for example, "Chapter Three: June 1995 Logic Game Setups." In addition, the Table of Contents lists the start page of each chapter. You can quickly find game setups within the book by referring to the top or bottom of each page, or by referring to the Table of Contents.

Grouping Game: Defined-Moving, Balanced

Employees: F G H K L

Positions: P M T

Possible Fixed Numerical Distributions:

P	M	T
1	2	2
1	1	3

1-2-2 Distribution:

1-1-3 Distribution:

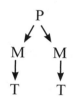

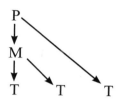

In the distributions above, the arrows indicate supervision assignments.

H, K, and L are all randoms, so your focus must be on F and G as you assess the game. Because F does not supervise any employee, F must always be a technician. Consequently, G is the only employee who has any restrictions, and these restrictions can be applied to the two distributions:

In the 1-2-2 fixed distribution, G cannot be a manager because each manager supervises only one employee, and the last rule indicates that G must supervise exactly two employees. Hence, in the 1-2-2 fixed distribution G must be the president.

In the 1-1-3 fixed distribution, G could be either the president or a manager. Because of the last rule, however, the supervision assignments are fixed: if G is the president, the G must supervise the manager and one technician, and if G is the manager, then G must supervise two technicians. Therefore, regardless of G's assignment, in the 1-1-3 fixed distribution the president always supervises exactly two employees and the manager always supervises two employees.

Question #1. Answer choices (A), (D), and (E) each violate the numerical distribution and are incorrect. Answer choice (C) is incorrect because F must be a technician. Accordingly, answer choice (B) is correct.

Questions #2 and #4. Both of these questions can be answered by examining the numerical distribution.

Question #5. Because F is a technician, only the 1-1-3 distribution allows F to be supervised by the president. Hence, answer choice (D) is correct.

Question #6. If K supervises two employees, and G supervises two employees, the employees must be in the 1-1-3 distribution, with G and K as the president and manager, not necessarily in that order. The other three employees are each technicians. Note also that answer choices (D) and (E) are identical.

February 1995 Game #2: Questions 7-12
Advanced Linear Game: Balanced, Identify the Templates

c: M P
g: W J
u: F K S

MP

K > S

Template 1:

c	c	g	g	u	u	u
M	P	W/J	J/W			
1	2	3	4	5	6	7

(below 5: S̸) (below 7: K̸)

Template 2:

u	u	u	g	g	c	c
			W/J	J/W	M	P
1	2	3	4	5	6	7

(below 1: S̸) (below 3: K̸)

The second rule creates two mutually exclusive sequences that produce the templates above:

$$\boxed{c\ c} \quad > \quad \boxed{g\ g} \quad > \quad \boxed{u\ u\ u}$$

or

$$\boxed{u\ u\ u} \quad > \quad \boxed{g\ g} \quad > \quad \boxed{c\ c}$$

These sequences are so powerful that you should immediately realize that the best approach to this game is to Identify the Templates. The two scenarios above provide sufficient information to easily answer most of the questions.

Question #10. Because K is a utensil, and K > S, if the utensils are washed 5-6-7 then K cannot be washed seventh. If the utensils are washed 1-2-3, then K cannot be washed third. Hence, answer choice (C) is correct.

Question #11. The condition in the question stem creates the following sequence:

$$K > \boxed{SF}$$

However, because K, S, and F are all utensils, they must be washed consecutively, and therefore they must form a block:

$$\boxed{K\ S\ F}$$

Accordingly, neither answer choice (A) nor answer choice (B) can be true. Answer choices (C) and (D) can be eliminated by applying the templates. Thus, answer choice (E) is proven correct by process of elimination.

Question #12. The condition in the question stem forces the objects into the first template above, with K washed fifth:

M	P	W/J	J/W	K	F/S	S/F
1	2	3	4	5	6	7

Grouping Game: Defined-Moving, Balanced

3 Goldfinches	2 Lovebirds	5 Parakeets
m: H	m: M	m: Q, R, S
f: J, K	f: N	f: T, W

___   ___   _____
Cage   Cage   Exhibition

Cage Rules\Deductions

J ←—+—→ K
Q ←—+—→ R
Q ←—+—→ S
R ←—+—→ S
T ←—+—→ W

Exhibition Rules\Deductions

S ←—+—→ J, W
S ——————→ T
S ←—+—→ Q, R
J ←—+—→ K
H, J, K ←—+—→ M, N

One of the initial rules states that birds that are both of the same sex and of the same kind cannot be caged together. Therefore, only one male parakeet can be assigned to each cage. Since there are three male parakeets and only two cages, it follows that at least one male parakeet must always be exhibited, along with a corresponding female parakeet. This inference is tested repeatedly.

Question #14. Since a pair of parakeets must be exhibited, and answer choices (A) and (C) do not contain a pair of parakeets, both answer choices can be eliminated. Answer choice (B) can be eliminated since J and S cannot be exhibited together. Answer choice (E) can be eliminated since W and S cannot be exhibited together. Consequently, answer choice (D) is correct.

Question #15. If Q and R are assigned to the cages, then S must be exhibited. If S is exhibited, then J and W must be assigned to the cages. Accordingly, answer choice (D) is correct.

Question #16. If T is assigned to a cage, then W must be exhibited since there must always be one male and one female parakeet on exhibit. If W is exhibited, then S cannot be exhibited. Since Q is assigned to a cage by the question stem, the only male parakeet that can be on exhibition is R. Hence, answer choice (D) is correct.

Question #17. We have deduced that at least one pair of parakeets must always be exhibited. In addition, one of the initial rules states that at most two pairs of birds can be exhibited at a time. Therefore, a pair of goldfinches and a pair of lovebirds can never be exhibited together, answer choice (B) is correct.

Question #18. If S is exhibited, both Q and R must be assigned to the cages. Accordingly, answer choice (E) is correct.

Advanced Linear Game: Unbalanced: Overloaded

Sports: H K M R V [5]

N ←—|—→ O

	M/R		R/M	
F				
W	V		H	
Sp		N̸/H̸		N̸/H̸
Su	K/M		V	

N ←—|—→ O

Because Otto's summer sport is V, and each child participates in four different sports, we can infer that Otto must participate in H during winter. And, because Nikki and Otto do not participate in the same sport in the same season, we can infer that Nikki must participate in V during winter. This inference is directly tested in question #19.

In addition, since H is only offered during the winter, Nikki will not participate in H during the year. This inference is tested in question #20.

Question #21 setup:

	R	M
F		
W	V	H
Sp	M/K	K/R
Su	K/M	V
	N	O

Question #22. Three of the four incorrect answers can be eliminated by applying the dual-options in the diagram at the top of the page. For example, according to the diagram, Nikki's fall sport is either M or R. Answer choice (A), which attempts to assert that Nikki need not participate in either M or R in the fall, can therefore be eliminated. Answer choice (E) can be eliminated because Otto has only three options for spring—K, M, or R—and answer choice (E) removes all three options. Answer choice (B), which eliminates only two of Nikki's three spring options, is therefore correct.

Question #23 setup:

	R	M
F		
W	V	H
Sp	M	K
Su	K	V
	N	O

Basic Linear Game: Balanced

H J K R S T [6]

HɈK

RꟻT

H > S

TɈJ and JɈT

The fourth and fifth rules combine to produce the following inferences:

$$T_3 \longrightarrow J_5$$

$$T_4 \longrightarrow J_2$$

The first inference is tested on question #2.

Question #3 setup:

H	J	S	T	K	R
1	2	3	4	5	6

Question #4 setup:

K	J/T	R	T/J	H	S
1	2	3	4	5	6

Question #5 setup:

H	J	S	R	K	T
1	2	3	4	5	6

or

T	H	J	S	R	K
1	2	3	4	5	6

Question #6. If H delivers the fourth speech, then J is forced to deliver his speech either second or fifth, and this violates the HJK not-block rule. Given that the only rule applicable to K is HJK not-block, you should be on the lookout for an answer that causes an HJK violation.

June 1995 Game #2: Questions 7-13
Mapping Game

The setup below is drawn from the PowerScore LSAT Logic Games Bible.

Planes: J K L M
Areas: R S T U

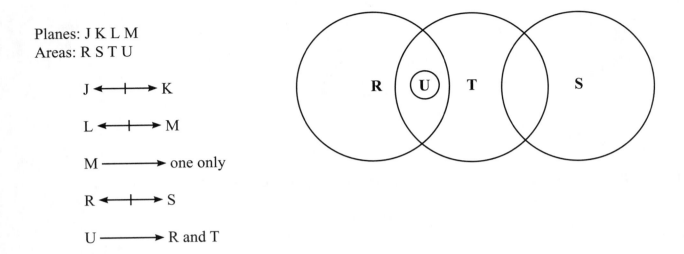

This is actually a Grouping game masquerading as a Mapping game. Especially indicative are the third and fourth rules, both of which are negative grouping rules. Since grouping is such an important principle on the LSAT, we felt it desirable to examine a game that has mapping elements but is controlled by grouping principles.

Although every student inevitably draws out the detection areas, it is probably easier to set this game up in a more linear fashion:

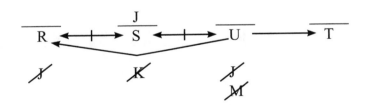

Note that the grouping rules involving areas R, S, T, and U are easily displayed within this diagram. Also, since the detection areas are now represented linearly, it is easier to utilize the Not Laws that apply to each plane. The game is now diagrammed in a much more familiar format and should therefore be easier to attack.

Question #7: Global, Could be true, List question. Answer choices (A) and (B) are eliminated since J cannot be in area R. Answer choice (C) is eliminated since M cannot be in area U. Answer choice (E) is eliminated since K cannot be in area S. It follows that answer choice (D) is correct.

Basic Linear Game: Unbalanced: Underfunded, Numerical Distribution

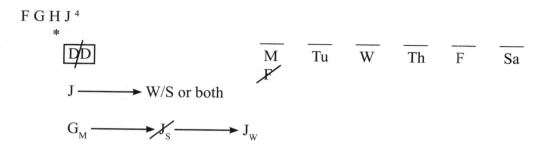

This game uses two unfixed numerical distributions for the 6 days to the 4 drivers: 2-2-1-1 and 3-1-1-1. The distribution directly answers question #17 and helps to answer question #19.

Question #16. If J drives on both Wednesday and Saturday and on no other day, then according to the last rule G cannot drive on Monday. Since F cannot drive on Monday, the only driver available to drive on Monday is H. Hence, answer choice (C) is correct.

Question #18. If G drives on Monday, then J must drive on Wednesday. According to answer choice (B), G drives on Monday and J drives on Tuesday. But, this creates a situation where J drives on both Tuesday and Wednesday, a violation of the second rule. Consequently, answer choice (B) cannot be true and is correct.

Question #19. If F drives exactly twice, but does not drive on either Tuesday or Wednesday, F must drive on Thursday and Saturday, and this forces J to drive on Wednesday:

$$\underset{M \atop \cancel{F}}{\rule{1.5em}{0.4pt}} \quad \underset{Tu \atop \cancel{F}}{\rule{1.5em}{0.4pt}} \quad \underset{W \atop \cancel{F}}{\overset{J}{\rule{1.5em}{0.4pt}}} \quad \underset{Th}{\overset{F}{\rule{1.5em}{0.4pt}}} \quad \underset{F}{\rule{1.5em}{0.4pt}} \quad \underset{Sa}{\overset{F}{\rule{1.5em}{0.4pt}}}$$

The diagram is sufficient to eliminate answer choices (C) and (D). In addition, because F drives exactly twice, we can determine that the drivers are in a 2-2-1-1 distribution. This information can be used to eliminate answer choices (A) and (B). By process of elimination, answer choice (E) is proven correct.

Another way to eliminate answer choices (A) and (B) is to realize that they are functionally identical, and any two identical answer choices must both be wrong because each correct answer choice is unique (the Uniqueness Theory of Answer Choices™)

Grouping Game: Defined-Fixed, Unbalanced: Overloaded

experienced plumbers: F G J K M [5]
inexperienced plumbers: R S T V [4]

F ⟷ M, R, V, T	EP\IP: __ __ __ __
J ⟷ R, T	EP: __ __ __ __
M ⟷ F	
R ⟷ F, J, S, T, V	
S ⟷ R, T, V	
T ⟷ F, J, M, R, S, V	
V ⟷ F, R, S, T	
T ⟶ G or K or Out	
R ⟶ G or K or M or Out	

The teams are not numbered since there is no "first" team or "fourth" team.

It is possible that two experienced plumbers could be assigned to one of the teams.

Question #20. Answer choice (A) is incorrect because K is an experienced plumber, and the question stem requires an inexperienced plumber. Answer choices (B) and (E) can be eliminated by applying the third rule. Answer choice (D) can be eliminated because according to the fourth rule T must be assigned with either G or K. Thus, by process of elimination, answer choice (C) is proven correct.

Question #21. Answer choices (A) and (B) can be eliminated by applying the second rule. Answer choices (D) and (E) can be eliminated because they both contain two inexperienced plumbers, a violation of the second rule (answer choice (D) is also incorrect because T must be assigned with either G or K). Thus, by process of elimination, answer choice (C) is proven correct.

Question #22. According to the fourth rule, T must be assigned with either G or K. If S is also assigned with either G or K, the only available plumber to pair with F is J. Therefore, answer choice (B) is correct.

Question #23 setup:

IP:	S	V	T	R
EP:	F	J	K	M

Question #24 setup:

IP:	R	S	T	V
EP:	M	F/G	K	J

Grouping Game: Defined-Fixed, Balanced

R S T V W X Y Z [8]

$$\frac{\boxed{\cancel{\frac{V}{Z}}} \quad \boxed{\cancel{\frac{S}{Y}}} \quad \boxed{\cancel{\frac{W}{Y}}}}{}$$

$$T_1 \longrightarrow Z_1$$

$$\frac{\underline{\quad} \quad \underline{\quad} \quad \underline{\quad}}{\underline{\quad} \quad \underline{\quad} \quad \underline{\quad}}$$
$$\frac{R \quad \underline{\quad} \quad S}{1 \quad\quad 2 \quad\quad 3}$$
$$\cancel{Y}$$

The combination of the second, third, and fifth rules leads to the following inferences involving W and Y:

$$W_1 \longrightarrow Y_2$$

$$W_2 \longrightarrow Y_1$$

The application of the final rule leads to a single solution:

$$T_1 \longrightarrow Z_1$$

$$\frac{Z \quad V \quad }{\frac{T \quad X \quad W}{\frac{R \quad Y \quad S}{1 \quad 2 \quad 3}}}$$

Because this rule is so limiting, you should expect it to be tested at most once or twice during the game.

Question #1 is a simple List question. The information from the hypothetical discovered in question #1 (namely that V can be added to class 2) can then be used to eliminate answer choices (A), (B), and (C) in question #2. the same hypothetical can be used to eliminate answer choices (C) and (E) in question #3.

Question #4 setup:

$$\frac{W/Y \quad T \quad }{\frac{V/Z \quad Y/W \quad X}{\frac{R \quad Z/V \quad S}{1 \quad 2 \quad 3}}}$$

The key to this question, and questions #3 and 5, is to Hurdle the Uncertainty™.

Question #5 setup:

$$\frac{W/Y \quad X \quad }{\frac{V/Z \quad Y/W \quad T}{\frac{R \quad Z/V \quad S}{1 \quad 2 \quad 3}}}$$

Advanced Linear Game: Balanced, Identify the Templates

Lions   Tigers

F G H J   K M

K̶		K̶
M		H

KJ

F/G	K	J
1	2	3

M	G/F	H
4	5	6

or

F/G	(G/F , M)	
1	2	3

K	J	H
4	5	6

The restrictive nature of the rules leads to the two templates above.

One of the mistakes made by many students is to misinterpret the KJ rule. The rule states that J is assigned to a stall numbered one higher than K's stall. Numerically, 2 is numbered one higher than 1, 3 is numbered one higher than 2, etc. Thus, if K is assigned to stall 2, then J must be assigned to stall 3.

Because a lion must be assigned to stall 1, and K cannot face H's stall, K can only be assigned to stall 2 or stall 4 (K cannot be assigned to stall 5 because that would not leave room for J). This means that the KJ block is assigned to stalls 2-3 or stalls 4-5. The two templates above are based on that inference.

This game can be somewhat difficult without the templates; with the templates, the game is easy.

This game is also the start of some interesting test construction elements used the test makers. Consider the following features of the second, third, and fourth games:

Game #2:   Features two rows, slots are numbered sequentially in horizontal fashion. Numerically, "2" is higher than "1," etc.

Game #3:   Features two rows, slots are numbered in non-sequential fashion (one odd row, one even row)

Game #4:   Numerically, "1" is higher than "2," etc.

In the second and third games, the slots are numbered in different ways, and in the second and fourth games, the numerical ranking relationships are opposite. These differences have the subtle effect of keeping test takers off-balance. For example, in the second game the slots line up 1-2-3, and in the third game they line up 1-3-5-7. Psychologically, it is difficult to develop a rhythm when the slots appear similar but are numbered differently. This type of construction is just another example of the psychological ploys used by the test makers.

September 1995 Game #3: Questions 13-18
Advanced Linear Game: Unbalanced: Underfunded

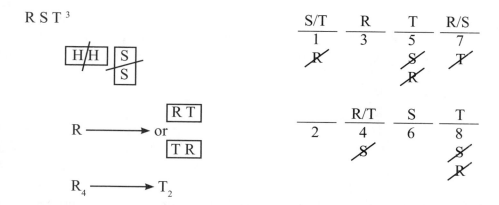

R S T [3]

The HH designation indicates that two Houses of the same style cannot stand next to each other. This representation is faster and easier than drawing out not-blocks for each style.

This is the easiest game of the test; the first two rules produce numerous Not Laws, and each results in a dual-option or style assignment. This greatly limits the possibilities of the game. One approach could be to draw out each possibility, but the setup above is so powerful that it appears that showing each solution would not be worth the extra time.

Question #15 setup:

S/T	R	T	R/S
1	3	5	7

R/S	T	S	T
2	4	6	8

Because this is a Could be True question, and only houses 1, 2, and 7 are uncertain, you should look for those houses in the answer choices.

Question #17 setup:

S/T	R	T	R/S
1	3	5	7

R/S	T	S	T
2	4	6	8

Question #18. This is a Suspension question, but, it is also a List question and so it is less time-consuming than other Suspension questions. In this question, answer choice (A) violates the third rule and therefore cannot be an accurate list of the styles of houses.

Pattern Game

R J S M L [5]

Odd		1	R
3 vs 2		2	J
5 vs 4		3	S
		4	M
Even		5	L
2 vs 1			
4 vs 3			

As with most Pattern games, this game has a minimal setup. See the Logic Games Bible for more information on Pattern game setups.

One of the critical inferences of the game is that one team does not participate in each round. For example, during an odd-position round, the team in position 1 does not play; during an even-position round, the team in position 5 does not play. Question #19 provides an excellent example of the usefulness of this information. If exactly one even-position round has been played, then L, the team in position 5, has not played and cannot have moved. Only answer choice (D) lists L in position 5, and thus answer choice (D) is correct.

A further application of the above inference occurs in multi-round situations. If you are given the order of teams in any round, then in the previous round for the first and fifth positions there can be only two possible teams that occupied that position: for position 1, the teams in position 1 and 2; for position 5, the teams in position 4 and 5. Question #24 uses this information to great effect. In question #24, the order of teams after three rounds is:

1	R
2	J
3	L
4	S
5	M

In attempting to determine the order of teams after the *second* round, it is important to realize that teams can only move up or down one position at a time at most. Thus, at the end of the second round either J or R *must* have been in position 1. Unfortunately, every answer choice lists J or R in position 1. Let us try position 5. At the end of the second round either M or S *must* have been in position 5. Because only answer choice (C) lists M or S in position 5, answer choice (C) must be correct.

Question #23. Only one hypothetical is required to solve this question. Either of these hypotheticals will work:

	even-odd-even			odd-even-odd
1	M		1	R
2	R		2	M
3	J		3	J
4	S		4	S
5	L		5	L

Basic Linear Game: Balanced

P Q R S T U W [7]

Q > W

U > P

$$\begin{array}{|c|}\hline R\ S \\\hline S\ R \\\hline\end{array}$$

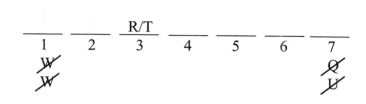

Question #2 setup:

Q	W	T	U	P	R/S	S/R
1	2	3	4	5	6	7

Question #3 setup:

$\boxed{T\ U\ R\ S} > P$

T	U	R	S	(	Q > W,	P)
Q	W	T	U	R	S	P
1	2	3	4	5	6	7

Question #4 setup:

$U > \boxed{P\ S\ R}$

U/Q	Q/U	T	P	S	R	W
		T		P	S	R
1	2	3	4	5	6	7

Question #5 setup:

$\begin{array}{c} U \\ \text{-----} > \boxed{P\ T\ W} \\ Q \end{array}$

Q/U	S	R	U/Q	P	T	W
Q/U	U/Q	R	S	P	T	W
1	2	3	4	5	6	7

December 1995 Game #2: Questions 6-12

Grouping Game: Defined-Fixed, Unbalanced: Underfunded

Off: F G H
Super: K L M

	H		
	G		K
Off:	F		
	P	Q	S

Two distributions of employees to committee assignments:

#1:	3-2-1-1-1-1
#2:	2-2-2-1-1-1

Question #8. If G is assigned to all three committees, then according to the fourth rule L will be unable to be assigned to a committee, a violation of the second rule. Accordingly, answer choice (B) is correct.

Question #9 setup:

	H	M	L/G
	G	G/L	K
Off:	F	F	F
	P	Q	S

Question #11 setup:

	H	L	L
	G	M	K
Off:	F	F/H	H/F
	P	Q	S

Question #12. If F and H are assigned to exactly one committee, then that committee is P. Consequently, G must be assigned to the other two committees, and G will then be assigned t all three committees. As shown in question #8, this is impossible. Hence, answer choice (B) is correct.

B L D S [4]
F H M O P [5]

S	$\underline{\quad O \quad}$	$\underline{\quad F \quad}$	(F, O)
D	$\underline{\qquad}$	$\underline{\text{H/M}}$	(F, H, M, O)
L	$\underline{\qquad}$	$\underline{\quad O \quad}$	(F, H, M, O)
B	$\underline{\text{P/H}}$	$\underline{\text{H/P}}$	(H, P, O)

$$V \longleftrightarrow W$$

Question #15 setup:

S	O	F
D	F/H	M
L	M	O
B	P/H	H/P
	V	W

Question #16 setup:

S	O	F
D	M/F	H
L	F/M	O
B	H	P
	V	W

Question #17 setup:

S	O	F
D	M/F	H/M
L	F/M	O
B	H	P
	V	W

J K L M N O P R [8]

```
P               4    O/    /O    R̸
V               3    P/R    N    J̸ M̸ Ø̸ R̸ L̸
R               2    K     L
                1    J/R   M/R   P̸ Ø̸ R̸ L̸ N̸
         J K——→X        Y←——M N L
```

The key inference of the game is that N must run third for team Y. This placement occurs because only P, R, and N can run third, but P and R cannot run at the same time. Hence, the runners for the third leg are N and the choice of P/R. This inference can be used to destroy questions #21, 22, and 23.

In addition to the N inference, there are several dual-options and split-options, and the game clearly has some inherent limitations. The best approach is to Identify all four Possibilities:

```
4    J    O        P    O        O    M        O    P
3    P    N        R    N        P    N        R    N
2    K    L        K    L        K    L        K    L
1    R    M        J    M        J    R        J    M
     X    Y        X    Y        X    Y        X    Y
```

This game serves as another example of a challenging game made considerably easier by showing all the possibilities or templates. Some of the "hardest" games on the LSAT are best attacked with these techniques, and once the correct technique is applied, the game no longer seems difficult. An examination of all LSAT games makes it clear that the test makers expect you to have the ability to identify "limited solution set" scenarios when they occur. In this game there are a large number of rules, and so it is not surprising that there would be some powerful inferences.

The setup below is drawn from the PowerScore LSAT Logic Games Bible.

F G H J Q R [6]

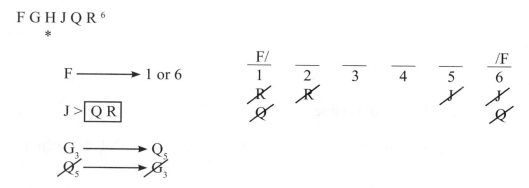

This game is perfectly Balanced, with 7 variables each filling one of 7 slots. The great benefit of doing Balanced games is that as you use a variable, that variable is knocked off the list and can no longer be used; when you fill a space, that space is unavailable to all other variables. In contrast, Unbalanced games have variables that can sometimes be used again (as in the fourth game in this set), and sometimes a space can contain two or more variables. This tends to make things much more confusing as all of the variables could be used again even if already placed once and spaces that contain a single variable might still be able to accommodate another.

An analysis of the variables reveals that H is a random, and this is indicated by the "*" notation. The first thing that jumps out regarding the rules is the linkage that can be made between second and third rule. This allows us to make a JQR super rule that yields six Not Laws (if you are unsure why a particular Not Law is given, attempt to place the variable in that space and observe the consequences). This should help you better understand why certain Not Laws appear). Furthermore, since Q appears in both the super rule and the last rule, we can make the following inference:

> If G is inspected on day 3, then Q is inspected on day 5 and R is inspected on day 6. Since R is inspected on day 6, F must be inspected on day 1. This inference leads to the further inference that only two possible scenarios exist when G is inspected on day 3: F-H-G-J-Q-R or F-J-G-H-Q-R.

The other issue to consider is the interaction between F and the Not Laws. If F is inspected first, then the Not Laws shift over one space, and R and Q cannot be inspected second, and R cannot be inspected third. The same logic in reverse can be applied to F in 6.

Rule Diagramming Note: The rule that states, "If G is inspected on day 3, Q is inspected on day 5" is conditional in nature and is represented with an arrow. The second diagram, with the slashes, is the contrapositive of the first diagram, and indicates that if Q is not inspected on day 5, then G is not inspected on day 3. Remember, the contrapositive of a statement is simply another way of expressing the original statement. The famous analogy we use is one that involves a penny: the two sides of a penny look different, but intrinsically each side refers to the same value. The same is true for a statement and its contrapositive.

June 1996 Game #2: Questions 8-12
Advanced Linear Game: Balanced, Numerical Distribution, Identify the Templates

LL☐ PP☐ RR☐ SS☐

LL☐ > $\dfrac{\text{PP☐}}{\text{RR☐}}$

The second rule produces a 2-2-2-1-1 unfixed numerical distribution.

The key to this game is to use the second and third rules to Identify the Templates™. Only two major templates exist:

1 possibility:

S	S		R	R
	L	L	P	P
M	Tu	W	Th	F

5 possibilities:

	S		R	
L	L		P	
M	Tu	W	Th	F

In the second template, the variety of possibilities results from the possible placements of the remaining S, R, and P workshops.

Grouping Game: Defined-Fixed, Balanced

Adults: F G H
       *
Children: V W X Y Z
                *

$$\text{Adults} = \begin{array}{cc} \rule{1.5em}{0.4pt} & \rule{1.5em}{0.4pt} \\ \rule{1.5em}{0.4pt} & \rule{1.5em}{0.4pt} \\ \text{X/Z} & \text{Z/X} \\ \rule{1.5em}{0.4pt} & \rule{1.5em}{0.4pt} \\ 1 & 2 \end{array}$$

$F_2 \longrightarrow G_2$
$G_1 \longrightarrow F_1$ (contrapositive)

$V_1 \longrightarrow W_2$
$W_1 \longrightarrow V_2$ (contrapositive)

When F is assigned to boat 2, G is assigned to boat 2, and since there must be an adult in each boat, H must then be assigned to boat 1.

$$F_2 \longrightarrow H_1$$

Similarly, when G is assigned to boat 1, F is assigned to boat 1, and then H must be assigned to boat 2:

$$G_1 \longrightarrow H_2$$

The contrapositive of these last two inferences:

$$H_2 \longrightarrow F_1$$

$$H_1 \longrightarrow G_2$$

Question #14 setup:

$$\text{Adults} = \begin{array}{cc} \text{Y} & \text{W/V} \\ \text{V/W} & \text{Z/X} \\ \text{X/Z} & \text{G} \\ \text{H} & \text{F} \\ \hline 1 & 2 \end{array}$$

Question #17 setup:

$$\text{Adults} = \begin{array}{cc} \text{Y} & \text{W} \\ \text{G/H} & \text{V} \\ \text{X/Z} & \text{Z/X} \\ \text{F} & \text{H/G} \\ \hline 1 & 2 \end{array}$$

Grouping Game: Defined-Fixed, Balanced

F G H J K L M N P [9]

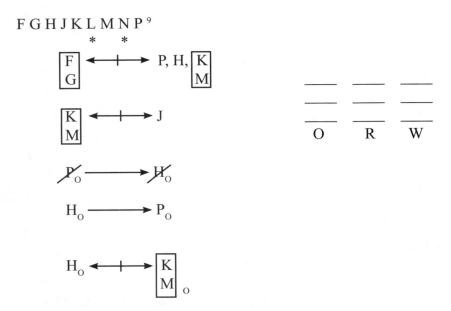

The difficulty in this game occurs in the large number of negative grouping rules you must remember.

Question #21. If M and P are both assigned to the Wetlands panel, K must also be assigned to the Wetlands panel. Since P is not assigned to the Oceans panel, via the contrapositive it follows that H cannot be assigned to the Oceans panel. Therefore, H must be assigned to the Recycling panel:

		P
		K
	H	M
O	R	W
H̶		

Question #23: If K and P are both assigned to the Recycling panel, M must also be assigned to the Recycling panel. Since P is not assigned to the Oceans panel, via the contrapositive it follows that H cannot be assigned to the Oceans panel. Therefore, H must be assigned to the Wetlands panel. Since the FG block cannot be assigned to the same panel as H, the FG block must be assigned to the Oceans panel:

	P	
G	K	
F	M	H
O	R	W
H̶		

Advanced Linear Game: Unbalanced: Underfunded

NO P R S T U ⁷ X X

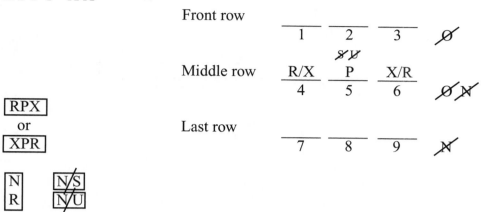

This game is Underfunded because there are only seven variables for nine spaces. Since each traveler can be assigned to only one seat, it follows that two seats will be empty. In order to more gracefully handle this empty space, you should create an "E" or "X" variable to indicate the empty space (in this case we chose X). This maneuver transforms the game from Unbalanced: Underfunded to Balanced. X is then treated like any other variable.

Note carefully that the third rule states that R's seat is the *row* behind the row in which N's seat is located. The rule does *not* say that R's seat is the *seat* behind N's seat.

Because the RPX block must be in the row behind N, and O is already in the last row, we can infer that the RPX will be in the middle row. Consequently, N must be in the front row.

At this point, from an abstract standpoint, the first three rules are well under control, or dead. The only active rule is the last rule, and you should be expect to be tested on the application of this rule. This last rule produces several Not Laws and inferences:

> Because N must be assigned to the front row, at least one of S and U must be assigned to the last row, and neither S nor U can be assigned seat 2.

> If N is assigned seat 2, then both S and U must be assigned to the last row.

> If S and U is assigned seat 1 or 3, then N must be assigned to the seat at the other end of the row.

October 1996 Game #2: Questions 6-12
Grouping Game: Defined-Fixed, Unbalanced: Overloaded

The setup below is drawn from the PowerScore LSAT Logic Games Bible.

G L M N P R S W [8]

$$GS \longrightarrow W$$

$$N \longleftarrow\!\!\!|\!\!\!\longrightarrow R$$

$$N \longleftarrow\!\!\!|\!\!\!\longrightarrow S$$

$$P \longleftarrow\!\!\!|\!\!\!\longrightarrow L$$

Exactly 2 of L, M, R must be reduced.

The selection of exactly five variables means the game is Defined-Fixed. Since there are eight variables from which to select, the game is Unbalanced: Overloaded.

The second rule bears further analysis. When N is reduced, neither R or S is reduced, and it can be inferred from the contrapositive that when R or S is reduced, N cannot be reduced. Thus, N and R cannot be reduced together, and N and S cannot be reduced together. Consequently, we have written the rule in two separate parts to fully capture this powerful information.

Because the last rule reserves two of the five spaces, it is the most important one. Any rule that controls the numbers in a game is always important, and this rule is no exception. If two of L, M, and R are reduced, then of the remaining five areas of expenditure—G, N, S, P, and W—exactly three must be reduced. And since N and S cannot be reduced together, the choice is further limited. On the diagram this has been represented with the two blocks. This separation of the variables into two groups is the key to making several powerful inferences:

1. Because two of the group of L, M, and R must be reduced:

   When L is not reduced, M and R must be reduced.
   When M is not reduced, L and R must be reduced.
   When R is not reduced, L and M must be reduced.

2. Because three of the group of G, P, W, N/S must be reduced:

   If G is not reduced, then P, W, and N/S must be reduced.
   If P is not reduced, then G, W, and N/S must be reduced.
   If W is not reduced, then G, P, and N/S must be reduced.
   (Later it will be discovered that W must always be reduced so this final inference will not be applicable)

Game #2 continued on the next page.

3. If G and S are reduced, then W is reduced. Since these three variables fill the reduction allotment of G, N, S, P, and W, it follows that when G and S are reduced, N and P are not reduced:

$$G\ S \longrightarrow W, \cancel{N}, \cancel{P}$$

4. When N is reduced, R and S are not reduced. When R is not reduced, L and M must be reduced. When L and M are reduced, P is not reduced. Thus, when N is reduced, R, S, and P are not reduced. Since there are only eight variables for five slots, when R, S, and P are not reduced, it follows that all five of the remaining variables must be reduced. Thus, when N is reduced, G, L, M, and W must also be reduced.

5. When L is not reduced, M and R must be reduced, and when R is reduced, N is not reduced. Thus, when L is not reduced, N is not reduced. By the same reasoning, when M is not reduced, N is not reduced.

6. When P is reduced, L is not reduced. When L is not reduced, M and R must be reduced. Thus, when P is reduced, M and R must also be reduced. This inference is tested directly on question #8.

Understanding how the two groups work—both separately and together—is clearly a powerful weapon against the questions. In this instance the groups are originated by the final rule, a rule concerning numbers. Always be on the lookout for rules that address the numbers in a game!

Question #6. Global, Could be true, List question. The application of proper List question technique (take a single rule and apply it to all five answer choices consecutively; take another rule and apply it to the remaining answer choices, etc.) eliminates every answer except for answer choice (A). Answer choice (B) is incorrect since both P and L are reduced. Answer choice (C) is incorrect since both N and R are reduced. Answer choice (D) is incorrect since G and S are reduced and W is not reduced. Answer choice (E) is incorrect because all three of L, M, and R are reduced. Consequently, answer choice (A) is correct. Of course, one of the most valuable results of answering a List question correctly is that we now know that the hypothetical G-L-M-N-W is a valid solution to the game.

Question #7. Local, Could be true, List question. Another List question, this time a Local question with the stipulation that W is selected. Do not make the mistake of thinking that because W is reduced that G and S are both reduced! This is a mistaken reversal of the rule. Answer choice (A) is incorrect since two of L, M, and R must be reduced and only M is reduced. Answer choice (B) is incorrect since both N and R are reduced, or alternately, because all three of L, M, and R are reduced. Answer choice (C) is incorrect because both P and L are reduced. Answer choice (D) is incorrect since both N and S are reduced. Consequently answer choice (E) is correct, and we now know that the hypothetical W-M-P-R-S is a valid solution to the game.

Question #8. Local, Must be true. As described earlier, when P is reduced, L cannot be reduced. When L is not reduced, M and R must be reduced, and hence answer choice (B) is correct.

Pattern Game

GOPRY [5]

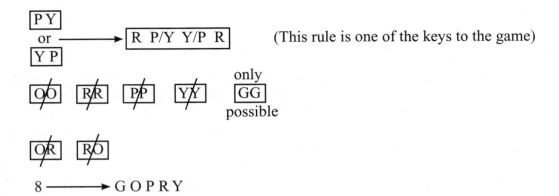

(This rule is one of the keys to the game)

The strand of beads has only a single direction and thus the last bead on a strand is *not* next to the first bead.

The final rule is easily misinterpreted. The rules states that any *portion* of the strand containing eight consecutive beads must include all colors. Thus, if a strand has 10 beads, then beads 1-8 must contain all colors, beads 2-9 must contain all colors, and beads 3-10 must contain all colors. Understanding this "portional" aspect of the rule is particularly useful on question #17.

Question #15 setup:

1	R 2	G 3	Y 4	O 5	P 6	R 7	8

(Below positions: under 1 — R̸/∅; under 5 — Y̸/P̸; under 8 — R̸/∅)

Question #16 setup:

P 1	Y 2	R 3	4	5	6

(Below position 4 — R̸/∅)

Question #17 setup:

P 1	Y 2	R 3	P 4	Y 5	R 6	G 7	O 8	9

(Below position 7 — R̸/∅)

Question #18. If the fifth and sixth beads are P and Y, then ultimately there will be no room for O among the first eight beads. Hence, answer choice (D) is correct.

Advanced Linear Game: Balanced

Songs: O P T X Y Z
Vocalists: G H L

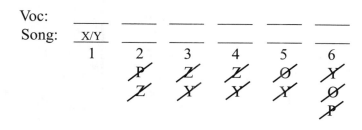

$$\frac{G}{XYZ} \quad \frac{H}{TPX} \quad \frac{L}{OPX}$$

$$Y_G > \overset{T_H}{\text{-------------}}$$
$$O_L > P > Z_G$$

$$1_V \longleftrightarrow 6_V$$

Y and Z must be performed by George, T must be performed by Helen, and O must be performed by Leslie. X can be performed by any of the vocalists.

Y must be performed first or second. Also, because the same vocalists cannot perform both first and last and George performs both Y and Z, if Y is performed first, Z is not performed last, and via the contrapositive, if Z is performed last, Y is not performed first:

$$Y_1 \longrightarrow \cancel{Z_6}$$
$$Z_6 \longrightarrow \cancel{X_1}$$

Question #21. From the Not Laws, only T, X, or Z could be the last song performed. Hence, answer choice (D) is correct.

Question #22. Since X is performed first, Y must be performed second, and answer choice (D) is correct.

Question #23. Answer choice (B) is correct since George performs both Y and Z, and the same vocalists cannot perform both first and last.

Question #24. If Y is performed first, then according to the inference above, Z cannot be performed sixth. Thus, P cannot be performed fifth and O cannot be performed fourth. Answer choices (A), (B), and (E) can be eliminated since each places O fourth. Answer choice (D) can be eliminated since the X-P-Z lineup violates the second rule.

December 1996 Game #1: Questions 1-6

Grouping Game: Defined-Moving, Balanced, Numerical Distribution, Identify the Templates

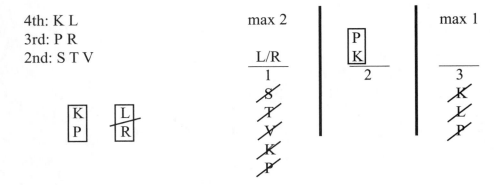

Only L or R or both could be assigned to singles; K and P must be assigned to a double; at most there can only be one triple.

The Numerical Distribution is hidden in this game. The singles, doubles, and triples form natural numerical limitations within the game, and then the assignment of students-to-rooms further limits the possible distributions. In fact, only three distributions of students-to-rooms exist :

Single/Double/Triple Numerical Distributions:

Distribution #1: 1-1-2-3

L	R	KP	STV
single	single	double	triple

Distribution #2: 1-2-2-2

L/R	KP		
single	double	double	double

Distribution #3: 2-2-3

KP	L __	R __ __
double	double	triple

Most of the questions can be easily answered by using the distributions above.

Basic Linear Game: Unbalanced: Overloaded

```
G G G
P P P                                        ___  ___  ___
Y Y Y                                         1    2    3
```

1P ———→ 2Y

2G ———→ 1G

3P
  or ———→ 2P
3Y

The contrapositive of the last rule is particularly important in this game:

$$2\!\!\!/P \longrightarrow \begin{array}{c} 3\!\!\!/P \\ \text{and} \\ 3\!\!\!/Y \end{array}$$

This is identical to saying:

$$\begin{array}{c} 2Y \\ \text{or} \\ 2G \end{array} \longrightarrow 3G$$

This information can then be added to the first two rules:

Rule #1:

$$[\, 1P \longrightarrow 2Y \,] \longrightarrow 3G$$

Rule #2:

$$[\, 2G \longrightarrow 1G \,] \longrightarrow 3G$$

In games such as this one with unusual conditional rules, always consider the contrapositives. For example, question #8 can easily be solved by taking the contrapositive of the second rule:

$$1\!\!\!/G \longrightarrow 2\!\!\!/G$$

Accordingly, if light 1 is Y, then light 2 cannot be G, and the correct answer is (A).

December 1996 Game #3: Questions 12-17

Advanced Linear Game: Unbalanced: Underfunded

Nonhostile: Q R U X Y Z
Hostile:

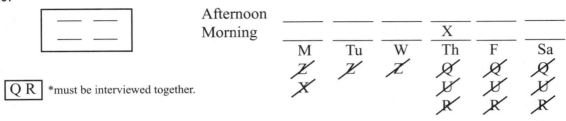

Since interviewing the hostile witnesses takes up two full days of the week, the hostile witnesses can only be interviewed on Monday and Tuesday, Tuesday and Wednesday, or Friday and Saturday.

The last rule states that Z must be interviewed after X, which is interviewed on Thursday morning. Thus, Z must be interviewed on Thursday afternoon, any time Friday, or any time Saturday. Therefore, if the hostile witnesses are interviewed on Friday and Saturday, Z must be interviewed on Thursday afternoon. Via the contrapositive, if Z (or Y) is interviewed on Friday or Saturday, the hostile witnesses must be interviewed either on Monday and Tuesday or on Tuesday and Wednesday. Essentially, if Z is interviewed on Friday or Saturday, hostile witnesses must be interviewed Tuesday and either Monday or Wednesday. This inference is one of the keys to the game.

Question #14. If Y is interviewed at some time after X, then Z must be interviewed on Friday or Saturday. It follows that Tuesday must be reserved for interviewing hostile witnesses.

Question #15. Since R is interviewed after Y, and R is interviewed before X, the following chain sequence results:

$$\begin{array}{c} Y \\ \quad > \boxed{Q\,R} > X > Z \\ U \end{array}$$

Since Y, U, and the QR block require three separate interview times, three of the six available interview slots during the Monday, Tuesday, and Wednesday scheduling period must be reserved for them. This effectively denies the hostile witnesses sufficient time to be interviewed during the Monday, Tuesday, Wednesday period and so the hostile witnesses must be interviewed on Friday and Saturday. It follows that answer choice (E) is correct.

Question #16. The conditions imposed by the question stem force the hostile witnesses to be interviewed on Friday and Saturday, and this forces Z to be interviewed on Thursday afternoon. It follows that answer choice (E) is correct.

Advanced Linear Game: Unbalanced: Underfunded

The setup below is drawn from the PowerScore LSAT Logic Games Bible.

There are seven products that must fill eight advertising periods (7 into 8). In order to compensate for this shortfall, exactly one of the products is advertised twice. This doubling produces a 2-1-1-1-1-1-1 numerical distribution. Regrettably, we cannot ascertain which product is doubled, and this greatly contributes to the difficulty of the game.

Since the products are advertised over a four-week period, and two products are advertised each week, our linear setup will feature two slots per week, diagrammed in stacks:

$$\frac{\underline{}}{1} \quad \frac{\underline{}}{2} \quad \frac{\underline{}}{3} \quad \frac{\underline{}}{4}$$

Note that you do not want to draw out the 8 spaces on one horizontal line. Having two stacks creates a vertical component and that allows for better representation of the different types of blocks (e.g. the HJ block versus the blocks involving G).

Using this setup, most students diagram the game in a manner similar to the following:

G H J K L M O [7]
　　　 * *

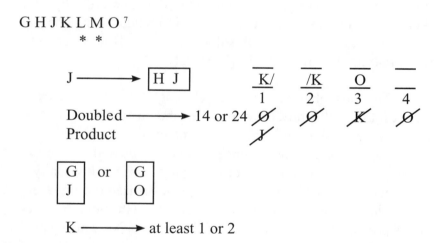

Several of the rules are quite tricky. The first rule, which states that "J is not advertised during a given week unless H is advertised during the immediately preceding week," can be partially represented as a block because of the "immediately preceding" qualifier. However, because of the "unless" portion of the rule (see the discussion of conditional reasoning on page 22), the block occurs only when J is present; hence, the rule is diagrammed as a conditional statement with an arrow. When J is advertised, H must be advertised in the preceding week; this automatically means that J cannot be doubled because this would cause H to be doubled as well.

Game #4 continued on the next page.

However, the normal Not Laws that follow from a block do not occur in this case because of the fact that one of the products is doubled (and thus the problems created by the Underfunded aspect of the game begin). While it is true that J cannot be advertised during week 1, it is *not* true that H cannot be advertised during week 4. Since H could be the doubled product, H could be advertised during week 1 and week 4, for example (J would be advertised during week 2).

The second rule also produces two notable inferences. Since the doubled product must be advertised during weeks 1 and 4 or weeks 2 and 4, any variable that appears in week 3 cannot be the doubled product and therefore could not appear in any week except week 3. By combining this inference with the last rule, we can infer that O cannot be advertised during weeks 1, 2, or 4. The second rule also allows us to infer that any product advertised during weeks 1, 2, or 4 cannot be advertised during week 3, since the doubling does not allow for week 3 to be used. By combining this inference with the rule involving K, we can infer that since K must be advertised during week 1 or 2 at the least, K cannot be advertised during week 3. K could still be advertised during week 4 since K could be the doubled product. Thus, a K Not Law cannot be placed on week 4.

There is still one critical inference yet to be uncovered, but because very few students discover this inference during the setup, we will continue on to the questions now, and then discuss the inference when it arises in question #20. The game diagram above is therefore only partially complete. We will fill in the rest of the diagram as we analyze the questions. We take this approach in an effort to more realistically deconstruct the way most students attack this game, and thereby provide more insightful and useful analysis. Of course it would be preferable for you to discover all inferences in a game before proceeding to the questions, but there will be times when this does not occur. How you react to that situation is just as important as your ability to make initial inferences.

Question #18: Global, Could be true, List. The most obvious rule to check first, O in week 3, does not eliminate any of the five answer choices. Either the third or fourth rules should be used next since they are the easiest to apply visually. Answer choice (C) can be eliminated since G is not advertised with J or O, and answer choice (D) can be eliminated since K is not advertised in week 1 or 2. Next, apply the first rule, because the application of the first rule requires less work visually than the second rule. Answer choice (A) can be eliminated since J cannot be advertised during week 1 and answer choice (E) can be eliminated since J is advertised during week 2 but H is not advertised during week 1. Thus, answer choice (B) is proven correct by process of elimination. Note also that by applying the rules "out of order," you save time because it is not necessary to apply the second rule, and the second rule would probably have required more processing time than the other rules since it forces variables to be counted.

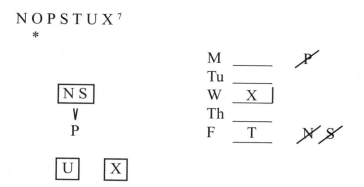

The difficulty in this game is generated by the unbalanced relationship of the variables to the number of days. Because there are seven variables and only five days, and each job takes either on full day or one half day, the following numerical distribution is produced:

$$7 \longrightarrow 5$$

2	2	1	1	1
N	(O, P, T)		U	X
S				

Because the rules assign jobs N and S to the same day, and U and X must take an entire day, we can infer that jobs O, P, and T must be done on the remaining two days, two jobs on one day and one job taking an entire day. Questions #5 and #6 test the Numerical Distribution inference involving O, P, and T (2-1 for these three variables):

Question #5. If P is not done on Friday, then P and T cannot be done one the same day. Thus, O must be done on the same day as P or T.

Question #6. If O is on Monday, it follows that P cannot be done on the same day as O, and thus P must be done with T on Friday.

Because N and S are done on the same day, and S must be done on an earlier day than P, thew following conditional inferences can be made:

$$P_{Tuesday} \longrightarrow NS_{Monday}$$

$$NS_{Thursday} \longrightarrow P_{Friday}$$

The inference involving N and S being done on Thursday is used to solve question #4.

Overall, this game is considered relatively easy.

Grouping Game: Defined—Fixed, Balanced, Identify the Possibilities

G H I K L M P [7]
   *

$$\underline{\hspace{1cm}} \quad \underline{\hspace{1cm}} \quad \underline{\hspace{1cm}} \quad \underline{\hspace{1cm}}$$
$$\quad T \qquad T \qquad T \qquad O$$

$M_T \longleftarrow\!\!\!|\!\!\!\longrightarrow P_T$

$K_T \longrightarrow M_T$

$G_T \longrightarrow H/I_T$

$H_T \longrightarrow K_O$

Inferences:

1. Combining the first two rules reveals that K and P cannot be on the same team:

$$K_T \longleftarrow\!\!\!|\!\!\!\longrightarrow P_T$$

2. Since the game has a two-value system (team or organizer), the contrapositive of the last rule produces a powerful piece of information:

Last rule: $H_T \longrightarrow K_O$

Contrapositive of last rule: $\cancel{K}_O \longrightarrow \cancel{H}_T$

However, if K is not the organizer, then K must be on a team, and if H is not on a team, then H must be the organizer. Thus, the contrapositive can be rewritten as:

Translation of last rule: $K_T \longrightarrow H_O$

Thus, the last rule reveals that either K or H must always be the organizer. This information should then be used to Identify the Possibilities:

Template 1:			
M	I	P	
K	G	L	H
T	T	T	O

Template 2:			
H	L/I	I/L	
G	M	P	K
T	T	T	O

Template 3:			
I	L/H	H/L	
G	M	P	K
T	T	T	O

The three templates above contain five separate possibilities. With these possibilities in hand, the game seems quite easy. But, without these possibilities, the game can be difficult.

Pattern Game

P Q R S T [5]

—	—	—	—	—
—	—	—	—	—
—	—	—	—	—
1	2	3	4	5

This Pattern game is a repeat of the fourth game of the December 1994 LSAT. The December 1994 version features five clans participating in annual harvest ceremonies.

As with most Pattern games, the setup is largely devoid of solid information, and there is no easy way to represent the rules.

The second rule is has a significant impact on the game: because the train stops at every station at least once in *any* two consecutive trips, if all the stations are known in any given year, then at least two of the stations are known in the preceding *and* following years. For example, if the train stops at stations P, Q, and R on the third trip, then the train *must* stop at stations S and T on the second and fourth trips:

—	—	R	—	—
—	T	Q	T	—
—	S	P	S	—
1	2	3	4	5

In addition, the rules produce a pattern in which each set of trips contains five distinct sequences. Each station must fit one of the sequences, and each set of trips must contain all five of the sequences:

$$1 - 3 - 5$$
$$1 - 2 - 4$$
$$1 - 3 - 4$$
$$2 - 4 - 5$$
$$2 - 3 - 5$$

Each station—P, Q, R, S, and T—fits one of the five patterns above, with each station fitting a different pattern. For example, consider the following hypothetical:

R	P	S	Q	T
Q	T	R	P	S
P	S	Q	T	R
1	2	3	4	5

In this hypothetical:

R fits the 1 - 3 - 5 pattern.
P fits the 1 - 2 - 4 pattern.
Q fits the 1 - 3 - 4 pattern.
T fits the 2 - 4 - 5 pattern.
S fits the 2 - 3 - 5 pattern.

Most people find this game quite difficult.

February 1997 Game #4: Questions 19-24
Advanced Linear Game: Balanced, Identify the Possibilities

F G H J K M [6]   Library: _____   _____   _____ ⨉ ⧸M⧹

                          Study: _____   _____   _____
                                   8   9   10
                                   ⧸F   ⧸H

G ≥ F

H > F

The GF sequential rule allows G and F to lecture at the same time. The HF sequence does not allow
H and F to lecture at the same time and hence F cannot lecture at 8 AM and H cannot lecture at 10
AM.

F is clearly a power variable in this game. Since F can only be placed in four different positions (9
AM in the library; 9 AM in the study; 10 AM in the library; 10 AM in the study), one effective approach to this game involves Identifying the four Templates based on F's position:

F in the library at 9 AM:

L:	H	**F**	K
S:	J/M	G	M/J
	8	9	10

F in the study at 9 AM:

L:	H	G	K
S:	J/M	**F**	M/J
	8	9	10

F in the library at 10 AM:

L:	(H , G/K)	**F**
S:	J/M	M/J	G/K
	8	9	10

F in the study at 10 AM:

L:	(H , G/K)	G/K
S:	J/M	M/J	**F**
	8	9	10

Overall, the game is very reasonable, and with the Templates, relatively easy.

The setup below is drawn from the PowerScore LSAT Logic Games Bible.

The first rule establishes that each table must have at least two sponsors seated at it, and since there are a total of seven sponsors, it can be deduced that one of the three tables will have three sponsors seated at it and the other two tables will each seat two sponsors each. This is a 3-2-2 numerical distribution. In this case, the 3-2-2 distribution is considered "unfixed," since the three sponsors could be seated at either table 1, table 2, or table 3. In some games "fixed" distributions occur, and these fixed distributions are generally a benefit since they limit the possibilities within a game.

The other rules of the game are relatively straightforward, and the initial setup should appear similar to the following:

K L M P Q V Z [7]
           *

Honors: K L M
Speech: M P Q

L
V

3-2-2 distribution:

___   ___   ___
_____ _____ _____
1   2   3

K̶
L̶
M̶
V̶

Since K, L, and M must sit at either table 1 or table 2, they cannot sit at table 3. Since V must sit at the same table as L, it follows that V cannot sit at table 3. Since K, L, M, and V cannot sit at table 3, only P, Q, and Z can possibly sit at table 3. Clearly then, table 3 is extremely restricted. As in any game, always examine the points of restriction since they often yield powerful inferences. In this case, since table 3 must have at least two sponsors, and only P, Q, and Z can possibly sit at table 3, at least two of the P, Q, Z group must always sit at table 3. Therefore, if a question states that one of the P, Q, Z group is seated at table 1 or table 2, then the remaining two sponsors must *automatically* be seated at table 3. Furthermore, any arrangement that attempts to seat two of the P, Q, or Z group at table 1 or table 2 will violate the rules and thus cannot occur. Ultimately, this simple analysis has uncovered the most important inference of the game. To reiterate, since table 3 has only three available sponsors to fill at least two seats, if any one of the sponsors is seated elsewhere, the remaining two sponsors must be seated at table 3. This is a variation of the type of inferences common when a dual-option is present, and you can expect at least one or two of the questions to directly test your knowledge of this inference.

June 1997 Game #2: Questions 8-14
Advanced Linear Game: Balanced, Identify the Templates

Sessions: M O R S
Psychologists: T V W
Nurses: F J L

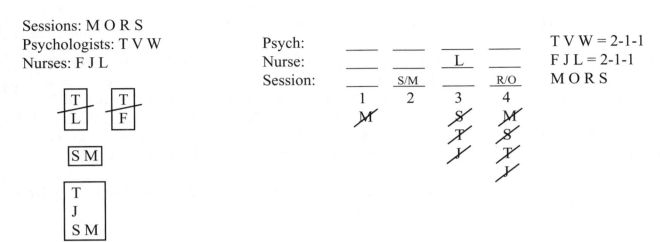

Since each psychologist must teach at least once, and the three psychologists must fill four teaching spaces, one of the psychologists must teach twice. The same is true for the nurses.

Since T cannot teach with F or L, T must teach with J. Since J must teach S, it follows that T, J, S, and M form a single large block. Since L must teach on day 3, the TJSM block must be scheduled for either days 1 and 2 or days 2 and 3. Further, since T and J are tied to S, and S can only teach once, it follows that T and J can only teach once.

Question #8. Since the question stem specifies that L teaches only once, F must be the nurse who teaches twice. Since the question stem also specifies that R must teach on day 3 with L, the TJS block must be scheduled for day 1 and M must be scheduled for day 2. Since J teaches on day 1 and L teaches on day 3, it follows that F must teach on day 2 and day 4. Since F does not appear in answer choices (C), (D), and (E), they can be eliminated. Since T must teach on day 1 only, answer choice (A) can be eliminated. Answer choice (B) is thus proven correct by process of elimination.

Question #9. The Not Laws easily answer this question.

Question #10. Again, the Not Laws easily answer this question.

Question #11. If S is scheduled for day 2, then T, J, and S must fill day 2 and M must be taught on day 3. Since L also teaches on day 3, L must be scheduled to teach M.

Question #12. If O and R are scheduled for consecutive days, those days must be day 3 and day 4. Thus T, J, and S must be scheduled for day 1 and M must be scheduled for day 2. Answer choices (C), (D), and (E) can be eliminated since they contain either J, or T, or both. Answer choice (A) can be eliminated since F and L are both nurses and two nurses can never teach together. Thus, it follows that answer choice (B) is proven correct by process of elimination.

Question #14. If O is scheduled for day 3, the dual option for the day 4 session indicates that R must be taught on day 4 and thus answer choice (A) is correct.

Advanced Linear Game: Unbalanced: Overloaded

Minimum requirements:

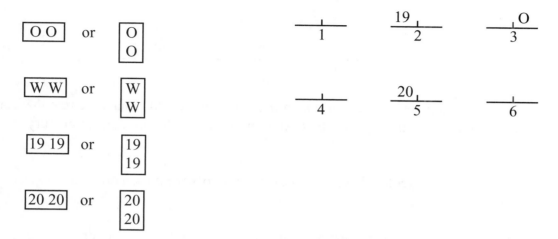

The setup to this game requires some manipulation. Since each of the paintings has two characteristics, oil or watercolor and nineteenth-century or twentieth-century, each of the paintings requires two separate spaces to represent these characteristics. In a normal linear game this could easily be represented by double-stacking the characteristics above each painting (as in most of the games in the Bible). However, since the paintings themselves are stacked into two rows, this would cause unnecessary confusion. Thus, we have chosen to represent the characteristics of each painting side-by-side. For example, 19O would represent a nineteenth-century oil painting, and 20W would represent a twentieth-century watercolor.

As with many games, this game utilizes several two-value systems. Since each painting must be either an oil or watercolor, but not both, if a painting is not a watercolor then it must be an oil, and if a painting is not an oil then it must be a watercolor. The same type of reasoning can be applied to the nineteenth- and twentieth-century paintings. This leads to several powerful inferences on question #15.

Question #15. The question stem states that all of the nineteenth-century paintings are watercolors, and this can be diagrammed as:

$$19 \longrightarrow W$$

The contrapositive of this rule would be:

$$\cancel{W} \longrightarrow \cancel{19}$$

However, because of the two-value system, if a painting is not a watercolor then it must be an oil, and if a painting is not a nineteenth-century painting then it must be a twentieth-century painting. Thus, the contrapositive above can be more effectively diagrammed as:

$$O \longrightarrow 20$$

Game #3 continued on the next page.

Question #15 setup:

19 ,W	19 ,W	20 ,O
1	2	3

___,___	20 ,___	20 ,O
4	5	6

Painting 6 cannot be a nineteenth-century painting since that would violate the rule that states that a nineteenth-century painting must be next to or below another nineteenth-century painting

Question #16. Since the two watercolors have to be next to or across from each other, all answer choices except (D) can be eliminated.

Question #17. If there are three oils, they must be paintings 1-2-3, paintings 2-3-6, or paintings 3-5-6. Thus, the watercolors must be paintings 4-5-6, paintings 1-4-5, or paintings 1-2-4. Accordingly, painting 4 must always be a watercolor and it follows that answer choice (C) is correct.

Question #18 setup:

,W	19 ,	,O
1	2	3

20 ,W	20 ,W	20 ,
4	5	6

Since there are only two oils, they must be paintings 2 and 3 or paintings 3 and 6. Thus, it follows that paintings 1, 4, and 5 are watercolors. Similarly, since there are only two nineteenth-century paintings, they must be paintings 1 and 2 or paintings 2 and 3. Thus, it follows that paintings 4, 5, and 6 are twentieth-century paintings.

Grouping Game: Defined—Fixed, Unbalanced: Overloaded

G H K L N P Q

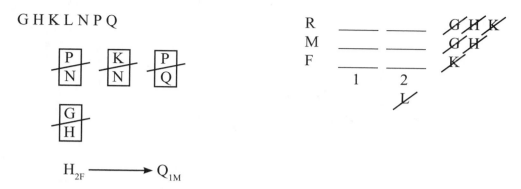

This game is quite difficult, in part because of the extra juggler available to fill the two groups, and in part because of the assignment of positions within each group. Note that if one juggler is unassigned, then the remaining six jugglers must all be assigned.

Question #21. If H is assigned to team 2, then Q must be assigned to the middle position on team 1. This fact eliminates answer choices (A), (B), and (C). Answer choice (D) can be eliminated since G cannot be assigned to the rear position on either team. Accordingly, answer choice (E) is correct.

Question #22. This extremely difficult question forces you to account for the variables remaining for team 2. In answer choices (A) and (C), the variables remaining for team 2 include pairs of variables which cannot go together according to the rules. In answer choices (B) and (D), the variables remaining for team 2 include H, but assigning H to team 2 forces Q into the middle position on team 1, which does not appear in either answer choice. It follows that both answer choices are incorrect. Thus, answer choice (E) must be correct.

Question #23. Similar to question #22, this question forces you to account for the variables remaining for team 2. If Q is not assigned on team 1, then H cannot be assigned to either team and all of the remaining variables must be assigned. This situation forces Q onto team 2, and L onto team 1, leaving K, N, and P for assignment to one space on team 1 and two spaces on team 2. However, no arrangement of the three variables exists that does not conflict with one of the initial rules. Thus, answer choice (E), the only answer choice to include Q, is the credited response.

Question #24. If G is assigned to team 1, and K is assigned to team 2, then only H, P, and Q remain to be assigned to the two available spaces on team 2 (N cannot be assigned to the same team as K, and L is never assigned to team 2). However, since P and Q cannot be assigned together, H must be assigned to the front position on team 2. Thus, according to the last rule, Q must be assigned to team 1. It follows that P must be assigned to the final position on team 2, the rear position. Answer choice (D) is thus proven correct.

Interestingly (in a demented way), this game ends with three vicious questions that require you to closely examine the variables *remaining* for assignment. Since it is so easy to get caught up in which variables have been placed, these three questions serve as a good reminder that in grouping games it is always important to examine the variables yet to be placed. Many of the most difficult grouping games have hinged upon recognition of this fact.

Basic Linear Game: Balanced

F G H J K L M
     *

$H > L > M$

~~HG~~ (boxed)

~~GH~~ (boxed)

$G_4 \longrightarrow H_1$

$$
\begin{array}{ccccccc}
 & \text{F} & & & & & \\
\hline
1 & 2 & 3 & 4 & 5 & 6 & 7
\end{array}
$$

(Not Laws under positions: under 1: ~~L~~, ~~M~~; under 3: ~~M~~; under 6: ~~H~~; under 7: ~~J~~, ~~H~~, ~~L~~)

Question #2. The condition in the question stem creates the following chain:

$$
H > L > M > \begin{array}{c} J \\ \text{- - - -} \\ K \end{array}
$$

Thus, H cannot be fill any of the final four tracks, and thus H must be first or third.

Question #3. From the Not Laws we know that neither L or M can fill the first position, and we also know F must be second. Thus, the remaining pieces—G, H, J, and K—could be first.

Question #4. The last two rules combine to create the chain sequence: $H > L > M$. Because H and L must both come before M, and F must be second, the earliest track that M can fill is the fourth position.

Question #5. The condition in the question stem creates the following chain:

$$GH > L > M$$

Since G and H form a block, the following setup results:

$$
\begin{array}{ccccccc}
 & & & \multicolumn{4}{c}{GH > L > M} \\
\text{J/K} & \text{F} & & & & & \\
\hline
1 & 2 & 3 & 4 & 5 & 6 & 7
\end{array}
$$

Overall, this game is considered very easy.

F G J K L M O

$$G_I \longrightarrow J_I \longrightarrow L_I$$

$$F_H \longrightarrow K_I$$

$$K_H \longrightarrow M_I$$

$$M_H + L_I \longrightarrow O_H$$

$$\overline{\underset{\text{Interviewed}}{F}} \qquad \overline{\underset{\text{Hired}}{}}$$

This game is difficult for two primary reasons: First, the number of applicants interviewed and hired is undefined. As mentioned elsewhere in the Bible, undefined grouping games are generally harder than defined grouping games because undefined games have a relatively greater number of solutions, and the lack of certainty in the setup forces the test taker to remember extra elements throughout the game. Second, the two groups are linked. Generally, grouping games feature separate groups with no true interrelation. For example, a game might feature children in separate canoes. Once a child has been placed in one canoe, he or she is then prevented from being in the other canoes and can be taken out of the variable pool. In this game, however, applicants who are hired must first pass through the interview group. Thus, an applicant who is placed into the interview group may or may not proceed to the hiring group. This effectively keeps variables "alive" even though they have already been placed once.

When diagramming the rules, it is important to use subscript designations for interviewing and hiring. It is also important to keep in mind the contrapositive of each of the rules. For example, the contrapositive of the fourth rule would state that "if K is not interviewed then F is not hired."

Question #6. The four incorrect answer choices can be eliminated by applying the first two rules.

Question #7. Answer choice (A) can be eliminated because F must be interviewed. Answer choice (B) can be eliminated because when J is interviewed, L must also be interviewed. Answer choices (C) and (D) can be eliminated because when G is interviewed, both J and L must also be interviewed. Since F is always interviewed, when G is interviewed at least three other applicants must also be interviewed. Answer choice (E) is thus proven correct by process of elimination.

Question #8. If M is not interviewed, then by contrapositive of the fifth rule, K is not hired. Accordingly, answer choice (E) is proven correct.

Question #9. The question stem specifies that six applicants are interviewed and three applicants are hired. In addition to F, since G must be interviewed, it follows that J and L must also be interviewed. Since F, G, J, and L take up four of the six interview spaces, only two of K, M, and O can be interviewed. This eliminates answer choice (C) since K and O would take up the final two interview spaces, leaving M out. But, according to the fifth rule, when K is hired then M must be interviewed, which is impossible given the conditions. Answer choices (A), (B), and (D) can all be eliminated by applying the last rule that states when "M is hired, and L is interviewed, O is hired." Since O does not appear in any of those three answer choices, they are all incorrect. Thus, answer choice (E) is proven correct by process of elimination.

Grouping Game: Defined—Fixed, Unbalanced: Overloaded

Anthro: F J M
Ling: N O R S

Anthro = ____ ____

Ling = ____ ____

$$1 \qquad 2$$

$$\boxed{\begin{array}{c}F\\\hline S\end{array}} \quad \boxed{\begin{array}{c}N\\\hline R\end{array}}$$

$$\boxed{\begin{array}{c}M\\\hline R\end{array}} \quad \boxed{\begin{array}{c}M\\\hline S\end{array}}$$

$$J_1 \longrightarrow R_2$$

Each team includes either one or two anthropologists and either one or two linguists.

Since M cannot be included with R or S, and each team must include at least one linguist, if M is included on a team then either N or O must be included on that same team.

$$M \longrightarrow N/O$$

Since S cannot be included with F or M, and each team must include at least one anthropologist, if S is included on a team then J must be included on that same team.

$$S \longrightarrow J$$

According to the last rule, if J is included on team 1, then R must be included on team 2. Since R cannot be included on a team with M, and because each team must have at least one anthropologist, it follows that if J is on team 1, then R and F must be included on team 2. Via the same reasoning, if R is included on team 1, then F must also be included on team 1.

Question #13. According to the last inference above, it can be deduced that if J is on team 1, then R and F must be on team 2.

Question #14. If N is on team 1, then R cannot be on team 1. Accordingly, answer choice (C) can be eliminated. Since team 1 must also include at least one anthropologist, answer choice (E) can be eliminated. Answer choice (A) can be eliminated since if J is on team 1 then F must be on team 2 (see the previous question). Answer choice (B) is difficult, but can be eliminated since if J and O are on team 1, then R and F must be on team 2. But if R and F are on team 2, then neither S nor M can be on team 2 and ultimately there are not enough researchers to complete team 2.

Question #18. If M is on team 2, then neither R nor S can be on team 2. Accordingly, answer choices (D) and (E) can be eliminated. Since R cannot be on team 2, via the contrapositive it follows that J cannot be on team 1. Since M is on team 2 and J cannot be on team 1, it follows that F must be on team 1 and answer choice (A) can be eliminated. Since F is on team 1 it follows that S cannot be on team 1. Since S cannot be on team 1 or team 2 it can be inferred that all other researchers must be included on a team. Accordingly, since J cannot be on team 1, J must be on team 2 and answer choice (B) is proven correct.

The setup below is drawn from the PowerScore LSAT Logic Games Bible

As with virtually all Pattern games, the setup contains little in the way of concrete information:

Q R S T U ^{5}

All = 1st or 2nd
5th ———→ 1st
4th at most once

Meeting 1: __ __ __ __ __
Meeting 2: __ __ __ __ __
Meeting 3: __ __ __ __ __
          1   2   3   4   5

Because the setup contains no "starting point" for analysis, the best approach is to review the rules in order to ensure a complete understanding of the game. As is often the case in Pattern games, the rules are difficult to diagram. However, it is important to symbolize the rules in some way since the focus of the game will be on their application. Fortunately, in this game the rules are relatively simple and thus easy to remember.

The first rule states that "Each candidate must speak either first or second at at least one of the meetings." Since there are three meetings, it follows that there are six available spaces for the candidates to meet this requirement. Since there are five candidates, each of which must appear once in these six spaces, it can be inferred that only one candidate can appear twice within the first two speaking spaces of all three meetings, and the rest of the candidates can only appear once. This is an unfixed numerical distribution of 2-1-1-1-1 for the six spaces that represent the first and second speaking slots of the three meetings. Essentially, this rule means that if one speaker speaks within the first two slots at two of the meetings, then the remaining slots must be filled with the rest of the speakers. For example, if Q speaks first at meeting 1 and second at meeting 2, then R, S, T, and U each speak once in the remaining first or second positions of the meetings. This inference comes into play on all of the questions, particularly questions #20 and #21.

The second rule states that "Any candidate who speaks fifth at any of the meetings must speak first at at least one of the other meetings." This is a powerful rule because it establishes a constant connection between the first and fifth spaces. Since the fifth space cannot be filled by the same candidate at all three meetings (that candidate would have to speak first at at least one of the meetings), it follows that there are always two or three different speakers in the fifth slot at all three meetings. If there are three different candidates speaking in the fifth slot, then those same three candidates will also speak in the first slot at a meeting in a different order. If there are two different candidates speaking in the fifth slot, then those same two candidates will speak in the first slot, with either another candidate in the remaining first slot or with one of the two candidates doubling up. Therefore, please note that if two different candidates fill all three of the fifth speaking slots, it is possible for a candidate to speak first at a meeting and not speak fifth. For example, if the fifth speaker at each of the three meetings, is R, R, and T respectively, then the first speaker at each of the three meetings could be T, Q, and R respectively.

Although the above explanation is complex, the application of the rule is much easier. Essentially, any candidate placed into the first or fifth slot immediately becomes subject to this rule. Combined with the first rule, slots one, two, and five appear to be the most controlling slots, thereby the most important ones.

December 1997 Game #1: Questions 1-5
Grouping Game: Defined—Moving, Balanced, Numerical Distribution, Identify the Possibilities

F G L N P S T

Appetizer-Main Dish Numerical Distribution:

Appetizer	Main Dish	
2	5	(2 possibilities)
3	4	(6 possibilities)

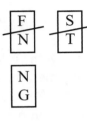

The first rule helps to determine the numerical distributions above. A 1-6 distribution is impossible because that would force either F and N or S and T together.

By combining the rules above, the additional inference can be drawn that F and G cannot be included in the same recipe together:

Because of the numerical distribution and the restrictive nature of the rules, this game can be attacked by Identifying the Possibilities:

2-5 Dist Possibility:

	P
	L
	G
F	N
S/T	T/S
A	M

3-4 Dist Possibility #1:

	L/P
P/L	N
F	G
S/T	T/S
A	M

3-4 Dist Possibility #2:

	L
N	P
G	F
S/T	T/S
A	M

There are only eight solutions to this game.

December 1997 Game #2: Questions 6-10

Basic Linear Game: Balanced

J K L M N O P [7]

K J

M > P

$L_3 \longrightarrow N_5$

~~P_2~~ $\longrightarrow P_5$

~~P_5~~ $\longrightarrow P_2$

	P/			/P		
1	2	3	4	5	6	7
~~J~~		~~P~~	~~P~~	~~M~~	~~P~~	~~K~~
~~P~~					~~M~~	~~P~~
						~~M~~

The last rule produces a situation where P must perform on either the second day or the fifth day. This rule, in combination with the third rule, produces the following inferences:

<u>Inferences:</u> $P_5 \longrightarrow$ ~~L_3~~

$L_3 \longrightarrow P_2$ and $N_5 \longrightarrow M_1 \longrightarrow K_6\ J_7 \longrightarrow O_4$

The second inference is quite powerful; when L is performed third, the entire schedule is determined: M-P-L-O-N-K-J. This inference is tested in question #7.

Question #8. The condition in the question stem produces the following setup:

	1	2	3	4	5	6	7
KJ in 6-7:	M	P	L/O	O/L	N	K	J
KJ in 3-4	M	P	K	J	N	L/O	O/L

Question #10. If J is scheduled second, the following scenario results:

1	2	3	4	5	6	7
K	J	L		N		

Under this scenario, there is no room for P, and thus the hypothetical fails. Thus, J cannot be scheduled second.

Overall, this is a very reasonable game.

Advanced Linear Game: Balanced

Int: F G H
Adv: X Y Z

$J_I > R_I$

$R_A > J_A$

| I_R / I_R |

Rosenberg:

Juarez:

Note that the setup above features separate groups of Not Laws for Rosenberg and Juarez. The Not Laws for Rosenberg below the Rosenberg stack, and the Not Laws for Juarez are at the bottom of the setup. The A and I sub-designation is the easiest way to keep track of the advanced and introductory textbooks since there are already two stacks for Rosenberg and Juarez.

Because Rosenberg cannot evaluate any two introductory books consecutively, and because Juarez must evaluate any introductory book before Rosenberg evaluates it, Rosenberg must evaluate the introductory textbooks second, fourth, and sixth. Correspondingly, Rosenberg must evaluate the advanced textbooks first, third, and fifth.

Juarez is not as limited as Rosenberg. For example, Juarez could evaluate the advanced textbooks second, fourth, and sixth, or fourth, fifth, and sixth.

Question #12 setup:

Question #13 setup:

Question #15 setup:

Grouping Game: Defined—Fixed, Unbalanced: Overloaded, Numerical Distribution

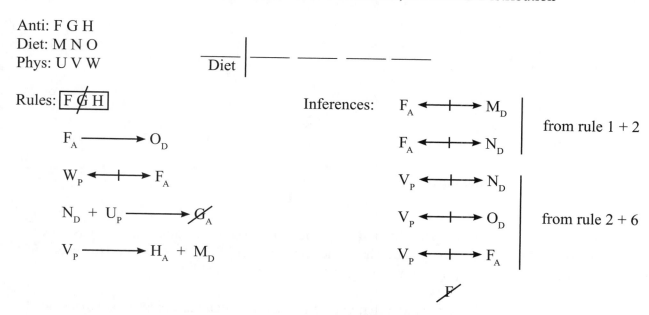

There are two numerical distributions in this game: 1-2-2 and 1-1-3.

In order to track the three treatment subcategories, subscripts are used.

This game contains a large number of rules and inferences which are tested throughout the questions. In fact, due to the restrictions there are only five solutions to this game:

> M-G-H-U-V
> M-G-H-V-W
> M-H-U-V-W
> M-G-H-U-W
> O-G-H-U-W

A student who identified each these five possibilities could easily destroy the game. However, because the game can so easily be solved by using the inferences, and identifying the possibilities is somewhat time-consuming, we do not feel it is necessary to identify the possibilities.

By applying the five not-block inferences above, the following answer choices can be eliminated:

> Question #18: Answers (A), (B), and (C)
> Question #19: Answers (A), (B), and (C)
> Question #20: Answers (B) and (D)
> Question #21: Answers (A), (B), (C), and (D)
> Question #22: Answers (A), (C), and (E)

Many of the remaining answers can be eliminated by a simple application of the rules.

Question #23. Don't forget to use the hypothetical from question #18 to help solve this problem!

Grouping Game: Partially Defined

F G H J K L M [7]
  * *   *

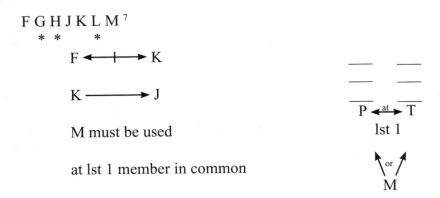

F ◄——|——► K

K ——————► J

M must be used

at lst 1 member in common

P ◄—at—► T

lst 1

↖ or ↗

M

This game would be classified as "partially defined" since each committee must have at least three members but possibly more. At first glance, the game appears as if it may be difficult. However, as you work through the questions, the game turns out to be fairly reasonable.

This game also serves as a useful reminder that you cannot assume that variables are always placed in exactly one group.

Please note that you *cannot* make the inference that F and J do not serve on the same committee together.

Question #3 setup:

```
         M
  L      L
  H      H
  G      G
  P      T
```

The setup for the trails committee contains the *minimum* number of members; there could be other members of the trails committee. The planting committee is complete.

Question #4 setup:

```
         M
  J      J
  L      L
  K      K
  P      T
```

The setup for the trails committee contains the *minimum* number of members; there could be other members of the trails committee. The planting committee is complete.

Grouping Game: Defined—Fixed, Balanced

Tourists: H I K L M N
Guides: V X Y Z
Languages: F R S T

$$K_X \longrightarrow M_{V/Y}$$

$$\frac{\quad}{V_F} \quad \frac{\quad}{X_{TS}} \quad \frac{\begin{array}{c}I\\H\end{array}}{Y_{FT}} \quad \frac{\begin{array}{c}L\end{array}}{Z_{SR}}$$

This game is made difficult because there are three variable sets: the tourists, the guides, and the languages. For the setup above, the guides were combined with the languages , and then the six tourists were assigned to the four guides. This "six into four" spread leads to two numerical distributions involving tourists-to-guides:

2-2-1-1

or

3-1-1-1

Since Y already has the assignment of H and I, we can infer that Y always has either two or three tourists, depending on the distribution:

$$2_Y\text{-}2\text{-}1\text{-}1$$

or

$$3_Y\text{-}1_V\text{-}1_X\text{-}1_Z$$

This distribution helps quickly answer questions such as #6, #7, and #8.

Question #9: According to the conditions in the question, K and L speak the same language. Since L speaks Spanish or Russian, K must speak Spanish or Russian and it follows that K must be assigned to X or Z. Since every guide must be assigned at least one tourist, this leaves only M or N to be assigned to V. Since V speaks French, it follows that M or N must speak French and thus answer choice (E) is correct.

Question #10: According to the conditions in the question, N and L speak the same language. Since L speaks Spanish or Russian, N must speak Spanish or Russian and it follows that N must be assigned to X or Z. Since the question asks you to maximize the number of Turkish speakers, you want to satisfy all conditions while at the same time maximizing Y. Thus, N should be assigned to X, and then K or M can be assigned to V, thereby satisfying the "one tourist to each guide minimum." Thus, we can achieve a 3-1-1-1 distribution with Y being assigned three tourists. Answer choice (B) is therefore correct.

Question #11: The conditions set up a 2-2-1-1 distribution wherein two of K, M, and N must be assigned to X and one of K, M, and N must be assigned to V. As such only answer choice (E) could be true.

Question #12: The following hypothetical proves answer choice (E):

$$\frac{K}{V} \quad \frac{\begin{array}{c}N\\M\end{array}}{X} \quad \frac{\begin{array}{c}I\\H\end{array}}{Y} \quad \frac{L}{Z}$$

Grouping Game: Defined—Moving, Balanced, Identify the Possibilities

K L M O P S[6]

$$M_G \longrightarrow P_G + S_G \qquad (M > P > S)$$

$$M_T \longrightarrow S_T \qquad (O > S > M)$$

$$P_T \longrightarrow K_T \qquad (K > O > P)$$

$$\frac{L}{G} \quad \frac{O}{T}$$

$$L > all$$

This game contains a two-value system: all players must play one of two alternate values, golf or tennis. Thus, if a player is not playing golf, he or she *must* play tennis, and if a player is not playing tennis, he or she *must* play golf. Applying this knowledge to the given rules leads to several interesting contrapositives:

$$P_T \text{ or } S_T \longrightarrow M_T \qquad \text{(contrapositive of rule #4)}$$

$$S_G \longrightarrow M_G \qquad \text{(contrapositive of rule #5)}$$

$$K_G \longrightarrow P_G \qquad \text{(contrapositive of rule #6)}$$

Since when M plays golf then S must also play golf (rule #4), and when S plays golf then M must also play golf (contrapositive of rule #5), we can infer that S and M always play the same sport. Thus, S and M form a block within the game. Since this block must be placed into either the golf group or the tennis group, two basic templates appear in the game:

Template #1:

$$\frac{S}{\underline{P}}$$
$$\frac{M}{\underline{}}$$
$$\frac{L}{G} \quad \frac{O}{T}$$

(golf: L > M > P > S)

Template #2:

$$\frac{M}{\underline{S}}$$
$$\frac{L}{G} \quad \frac{O}{T}$$

(tennis: O > S > M)

In template #1, K is the only variable yet to be placed and there are no restrictions on its placement.

In template #2, K and P are the only variables yet to be placed. According to the rules, if K plays golf, then P plays golf, and if P plays tennis then K plays tennis.

These two basic templates provide a solid base with which to attack the questions. The biggest issue then becomes the ordering of the players within each sport.

3 variable sets: order, song, song type

Ballads: F G H
Dance: R S V X

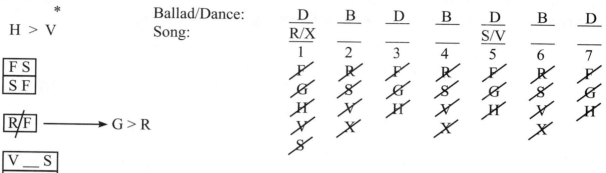

H > V

This game features the Separation Principle™. The Separation Principle applies when variables involved in not-blocks are placed into a limited number of spaces. For example, suppose two boys are placed into three chairs, with a rule that the two boys cannot sit next to one another. The minimum amount of room needed to comply with the not-block rule is:

$$\boxed{\text{B} \ \_\_\_ \ \text{B}}$$

Since the minimum requirement happens to be the same as the number of available spaces, the boys are forced into spaces 1 and 3:

$$\frac{\text{B}}{1} \quad \frac{\phantom{\text{B}}}{2} \quad \frac{\text{B}}{3}$$

Now suppose we expand the scenario to four boys being placed into seven chairs, still with the rule that no boys can sit next to each other. The minimum space required by the not-block rule is:

$$\boxed{\text{B} \ \_\_ \ \text{B} \ \_\_ \ \text{B} \ \_\_ \ \text{B}}$$

Again, the minimum requirement happens to be identical to the number of available spaces, and the boys are forced into spaces 1, 3, 5, and 7:

$$\frac{\text{B}}{1} \quad \frac{\phantom{\text{B}}}{2} \quad \frac{\text{B}}{3} \quad \frac{\phantom{\text{B}}}{4} \quad \frac{\text{B}}{5} \quad \frac{\phantom{\text{B}}}{6} \quad \frac{\text{B}}{7}$$

This scenario is, of course, identical to the one in this game, with the boys representing the dance tunes.

Advanced Linear Game: Balanced

The setup below is drawn from the PowerScore LSAT Logic Games Bible.

In this Defined, Balanced game there are three variable sets: the four majors, the four nonmajors, and the four laboratory benches. Since the laboratory benches have a sense of order, they should be selected as the base. A diagram similar to the following should be created:

Majors: F G H J ^{4}
Nonmajors: V W X Y ^{4}

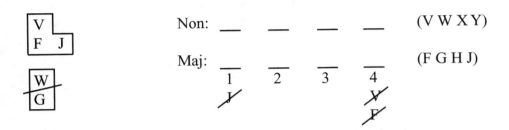

The second rule can be somewhat confusing. "Lower-numbered" mean one number is less than another; for example, 2 is less than 3. Do not confuse the meaning of this rule with ranking-type games where 1 is ranked higher than 2, etc. (games like this *do* occur on the LSAT). When the rule discusses "lower-numbered" or "higher-numbered" elements, it means actual numerical value and 1 is always lower than 2, 2 is always lower than 3, 3 is always lower than 4, and so on. Thus the rule is properly diagrammed as an FJ block. Applying the basic principle of linkage to the second and third rules produces the VFJ super-block. This super block is clearly one of the keys to the game since it has a limited number of placement options. In fact, the game is made somewhat easier by the fact that there are only two "active" rules to track: the VFJ super-block and the GW not-block. The first rule is essentially dead since it is incorporated into the main setup. With only two active rules to consider, you should always be looking to apply them as you attack the questions.

The setup below is drawn from the PowerScore LSAT Logic Games Bible.

L M N O P S T⁷
          *

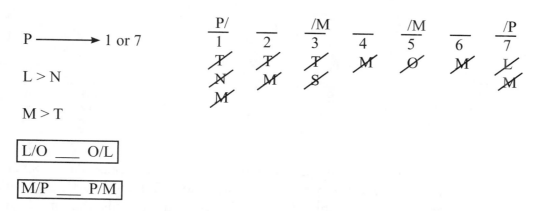

P ——→ 1 or 7

L > N

M > T

| L/O ___ O/L |

| M/P ___ P/M |

This game is perfectly Balanced, with 7 variables each filling one of 7 slots. The first inference that can be made comes from the linkage of M and P. Since P must be delivered first or seventh, and exactly one package is delivered between P and M, it follows that M must be delivered third or fifth. Therefore, M cannot be delivered first, second, fourth, sixth or seventh. Since the earliest M can be delivered is third, that affects the delivery of T, and it can be inferred that T cannot be delivered first, second, or third.

Two other Not Laws also bear further examination. First, S cannot be delivered third because it sets off a the following chain: M would be delivered fifth and P would be delivered seventh; in turn L and O have to be delivered second and fourth, with L being delivered second; this causes a problem since there is no room for N, which must be delivered after L. Second, O cannot be delivered fifth because of the problems it causes: M would have to be delivered third and P would have to be delivered first; since O and L must be separated by one package, L would have to be delivered seventh, and that is impossible since L must be delivered ahead of N.

Additionally, since the MP block is reduced to exactly two spacing options, one approach to setting up the game involves drawing out the two options, which are labeled #1 and #2 below:

	1	2	3	4	5	6	7
#1:	__	__	__	__	M	T	P
#2:	P	__	M	__	__	__	__

In option #1, we can link rules and apply the M > T rule, which yields the inference that T must be sixth when P is seventh and M is fifth. At this point, it should be apparent that you will have to keep an eye on L, N, and O since they are linked together. In general, the variables L, M, and P are the most powerful since each appears in two separate rules.

Grouping Game: Defined—Moving, Balanced, Numerical Distribution, Identify the Possibilities

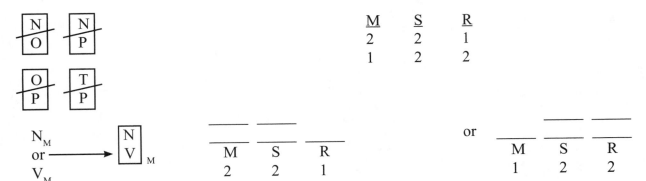

N O P T V [5]   Two Numerical Distributions:

P is the most restricted, and thus the most important, variable in the game. Because P cannot participate in the same activity as N, O, or T, if P participates in a group of 2, P must participate with V. Otherwise, P is alone. This restriction, in combination with the two numerical distributions, leads to the decision to Identify the Possibilities:

P goes to a movie, 1-2-2 distribution:

	T/V	V/T
P	N/O	O/N
M	S	R

P goes to a soccer game, 2-2-1 distribution:

	T		V	
	O		P	N
	M		S	R

P goes to a soccer game, 1-2-2 distribution:

	V	T
O	P	N
M	S	R

P goes to a restaurant, 2-2-1 distribution, N and V go to a movie:

	N		O	
	V		T	P
	M		S	R

P goes to a restaurant, 1-2-2 distribution:

	T	V
O	N	P
M	S	R

P goes to a restaurant, 2-2-1 distribution, N and V go to a soccer game:

	O		N	
	T		V	P
	M		S	R

The last rule has a great impact on the possibilities above. For example, if P goes to a movie, P must go alone (otherwise the NV movie rule will apply because P would be with V). Thus, P can only go to a movie in the 1-2-2 distribution. In addition, in a number of the possibilities, when P and V participate in the same activity, then N cannot go to a movie and must instead go to a soccer game or a restaurant.

Grouping Game: Defined—Fixed, Unbalanced: Overloaded, Identify the Possibilities

law: F G H I

sci: V Y Z

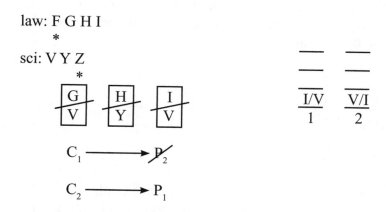

$$C_1 \longrightarrow \cancel{P_2}$$

$$C_2 \longrightarrow P_1$$

Since V appears in two of the three rules, V is a logical starting point for our analysis. If V serves on a panel, then neither G nor I can serve on that panel. Because exactly two lawmakers must serve on the panel, it follows that if V serves on a panel, then F and H must serve on that panel:

$$V \longrightarrow F, H$$

Of course, if H serves on the panel, then Y cannot serve on that panel:

$$V \longrightarrow F, H \longrightarrow \cancel{Y}$$

Because Y cannot serve on the panel, and there must be two scientists on the panel, Z must serve on the panel:

$$V \longrightarrow F, H \longrightarrow \cancel{Y} \longrightarrow Z$$

This is an extremely important inference because of the rule that states that each year either I or V serves on the panel. When V serves on the panel, the other three members are *always* F, H, and Z. This relationship pattern also reveals an underlying inference of the game: because V and Y can never serve together, we can infer that Z must always serve on the panel. This inference is tested in question #24.

The panel membership is also restricted when I serves on the panel. Because I cannot serve with V, and there must be two scientists, when I serves on the panel we can infer that Y and Z serve on the panel. And, when because H and Y cannot serve together, the remaining member is F or G. Thus, when I serves on the panel, the remaining members are *always* Y, Z, and F or G.

Because I or V, but not both, serve on each panel, there are initially four possible combinations:

1. I serves on the panel in the first year, V serves on the panel in the second year.
2. V serves on the panel in the first year, I serves on the panel in the second year.
3. I serves on the panel in both years.
4. V serves on the panel in both years.

Game #4 continued on the next page.

However, if V serves on both panels, the rule stating that the chairperson in the first year cannot serve on the panel in the second year is violated. Thus, there are only three combinations of I and V, and the game should be attacked by Identifying the Possibilities:

$$
\begin{array}{cc}
Z & H \\
\hline
Y & F \\
\hline
F/G & Z \\
\hline
I & V \\
\hline
1 & 2
\end{array}
\qquad
\begin{array}{cc}
H & Z \\
\hline
F & Y \\
\hline
Z & F/G \\
\hline
V & I \\
\hline
1 & 2
\end{array}
\qquad
\begin{array}{cc}
Z & Z \\
\hline
Y & Y \\
\hline
F/G & G/F \\
\hline
I & I \\
\hline
1 & 2
\end{array}
$$

The three templates above encompass the only six solutions of the game. The only remaining consideration is the chairperson of each panel. For example, the third template will work only if F or G is the chairperson in the first year. If F is the chairperson in the first year, then G must serve on the panel in the second year, and I, Y, or Z is the chairperson in the second year; If G is the chairperson in the first year, then F must serve on the panel in the second year, and I, Y, or Z is the chairperson in the second year.

Overall, the game is very difficult. The Identify the Possibilities technique makes the game manageable, but it requires some insight in order to apply the technique.

Basic Linear Game: Balanced

F G H J K L M ^{7}
          *

$\boxed{\text{H G}}$

		F/		/F		
___	___	___	___	___	___	___
1	2	3	4	5	6	7

$K_4 \longrightarrow L_5 \longrightarrow F_3 \longrightarrow \cancel{K_1} \ \cancel{G}$

$F_5 \longrightarrow \cancel{K_4}$

$J_1 \longrightarrow$ Only one possibility: J-H-G-M-F-K-L

Question #2 setup:

J	H	G	M	F	K	L
1	2	3	4	5	6	7

Question #3 setup:

H	G	F	K	L	J	M
1	2	3	4	5	6	7

Question #5 setup:

M	L	F	J	K	H	G
1	2	3	4	5	6	7

Question #6. The conditions imposed by the question stem produce the following sequence:

$\boxed{\text{HG}}$
- - - > F
L

Accordingly, F cannot view the site on day 3, and therefore F must view the site on day 5. Because H, G, and L must all view the site before F, an inference can made that either H, G, or L must view the site on day 3. If H, G, or L does not view the site on day 3, then H and G view the site on day 1 and 2, respectively, and the only remaining day for L to view the site is day 4, a violation of the second rule. Among the answer choices, only answer choice (B) lists one of the three investors H, G, or L, and therefore answer choice (B) is correct.

December 1998 Game #2: Questions 7-12

Grouping/Linear Combination Game, Numerical Distribution, Identify the Templates

S S S S ^{4}

L L L ^{3}

	1	2	3	4	5

F F F F F ^{5}

M M ^{2}

At Lst 2 FS

At Lst 1 FL

<u>Numerical Distributions</u>

	#1:	2	2	1	1	1
		S	S	L	L	L
		S	S	S		

L̸/S

or

FS /̸ ML		S	L	S	S	L
		S	L			

ML /̸ FS

	#2:	2	2	2	1	0
		S	S	L	L	
		S	S	L		

In addition, the Overlap Principle can be applied to the male/female and snakes/lizards relationship:

> Because there are only two males, the maximum number of male snakes (MS) is two. Yet, there are four snakes total, so, at a minimum, there must be at least two female snakes (FS).

> The same reasoning can be applied to the relationship of the males and the lizards. Because there are only two males, the maximum number of male lizards (ML) is two. Yet, there are three lizards total, so, at a minimum, there must be at least one female lizard (FL).

The inference that there are at least two FS and at least one FL can be used to identify the three possible male/female and snake/lizard combinations:

Possibility #1:   FS, FS, FL   FS, FS, ML, ML

Possibility #2:   FS, FS, FL   FL, FL, MS, MS

Possibility #3:   FS, FS, FL   FS, FL, MS, ML

Even with all of the information above, this remains a very difficult game.

December 1998 Game #3: Questions 13-19
Grouping Game: Defined—Moving, Balanced, Numerical Distribution, Identify the Templates

The setup below is drawn from the PowerScore LSAT Logic Games Bible.

The information in the game scenario establishes that there are seven film buffs attending a showing of three movies. Each film buff sees exactly one film. The first rule establishes two fixed distributions:

	Fellini	Hitchcock	Kurosawa
Fixed Distribution #1:	1	2	4
Fixed Distribution #2:	2	4	1

The two fixed distributions create two distinctly different scenarios. And since each scenario requires a different analysis, the best strategy is to create two templates, one for the 1-2-4 distribution, and another for the 2-4-1 distribution:

```
   1     2     4              2     4     1

              ___                  ___
              ___                  ___
        ___   ___            ___   ___
   ___  ___   ___            ___   ___   ___
    F    H     K              F     H     K
```

The rules can now be considered:

G I L M R V Y [7]

```
 ┌───┐  ┌───┐  ┌───┐
 │ G │  │ I │  │ V │
 ├───┤  ├───┤  │ Y │
 │ R │  │ M │  └───┘
 └───┘  └───┘
```

Of course, the rules impact each template:

```
   1     2     4              2     4     1

              I/M
              R/G                  Y
              Y                    V
        ___   V            ___     L     /G
   G/   L     V            G/      L     /G
   F    H     K            F       H     K
         Ø                         Ø
```

Basic Linear Game: Balanced, Identify the Possibilities

G G O O P P [6]

P/G			P/O	P/	/P
1	2	3	4	5	6
∅	∅		∅		

C/C

The C designation in the not-block above stands for "car." The CC not-block is a shorthand notation that indicates that no two cars of similar color can be adjacent, as required by the first rule. This representation saves the time of writing out PP, GG, and OO not-blocks.

The rule that states that Car 1 cannot be orange leads to the important Not Law that Car 2 cannot be green. Let's examine why this is the case, using the two scenarios for Car 1:

1. <u>Car 1 is green</u>. If Car 1 is green, then Car 2 cannot be green.

2. <u>Car 1 is purple</u>. When Car 1 is purple, then Car 5 or 6 is also purple, and we can deduce that Car 4 is orange. When Car 4 is orange, then Car 3 cannot be orange (from the rule that no two adjacent cars can be of the same color) and Car 3 cannot be purple (because the two purple cars are either 1-5 or 1-6). Consequently, Car 3 must be green. And, when Car 3 is green, Car 2 cannot be green.

Thus, regardless of whether Car 1 is purple or green, Car 2 can never be green.

An analysis of the diagram above reveals that the placement of the two P cars is restricted. It makes sense to attack the game by Identifying the Possibilities:

Three possibilities with P in 6:

#1:	G	O	G	P	O	P
#2:	P	O	G	O	G	P
#3:	G	O	P	O	G	P

Three possibilities with P in 5:

#4:	G	P	G	O	P	O
#5:	P	O	G	O	P	G
#6:	G	O	P	O	P	G

With these solutions in hand, the questions are easy to attack.

Basic Linear Game: Balanced, Identify the Templates

K L M N O P [7]

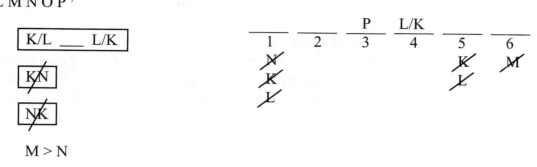

The L and K split-block is clearly the most restricted element in the game. Because P is assigned to position 3, the LK block must be assigned to positions 2 and 4, or positions 4 and 6. This restriction, in combination with the remaining rules, suggests Identifying the Templates:

	1	2	3	4	5	6
Template #1:	M	N	P	K/L	O	L/K
Template #2:	M/O	K/L	P	L/K	(O/M,	N)

If the two templates above are confusing, another option would be to Identify the Possibilities:

L in 4, K in 6:

	1	2	3	4	5	6	
Possibility #1:	M	N	P	L	O	K	(1 solution)

K in 4, L in 6:

	1	2	3	4	5	6	
Possibility #2:	M	N	P	K	O	L	(1 solution)

K in 2, L in 4:

	1	2	3	4	5	6	
Possibility #3:	M/O	K	P	L	O/M	N	(2 solutions)
Possibility #4:	M/O	K	P	L	N	O/M	(2 solutions)

L in 2, K in 4:

	1	2	3	4	5	6	
Possibility #5:	M/O	L	P	K	O/M	N	(2 solutions)

There are eight total possibilities.

June 1999 Game #2: Questions 6-12
Grouping Game: Defined—Fixed, Unbalanced: Underfunded

The setup below is drawn from the PowerScore LSAT Logic Games Bible.

When you create this setup, it is critical that the correct base be selected. There are two choices: the four researchers or the four languages. Since the researchers can learn one to three languages but it is uncertain exactly how many languages each researcher learns, the researchers seem a poor choice for the base. On the other hand, the number of researchers learning each language is clearly specified in the rules and as such the languages are the best choice for the base:

$$\overline{}$$
$$\overline{}\quad\overline{}\quad\overline{}$$
$$\overline{\text{R}}\quad\overline{\text{S}}\quad\overline{\text{T}}\quad\overline{\text{Y}}$$

The distribution of researchers to languages is thus fixed at 1-2-2-3, and since there are only four researchers, it is clear that at least two researchers will have to learn more than one language (in fact, at least two researchers and at most three researchers will learn more than one language). Using the above base, we can set up the game as follows:

G H L P ^{4}

G ⟶ H

3 ≥ R ≥ 1

From the rules it is clear that G is a power variable, since G appears in both the non-numerical rules. The key inference involving G comes with Yoruba. Because Yoruba must be learned by exactly three researchers, and G cannot be selected with either L or P, it can be inferred that G cannot learn Yoruba, and the other three researchers must learn Yoruba. Additionally, since when G is selected H must also be selected, it is not possible for G to learn Rundi, as there is no room for H to be selected. Consequently, since G must learn at least one language, G (in the form of a GH block) must learn either Swahili or Tigrinya or both. From this inference it follows that neither L nor P can learn *both* Swahili and Tigrinya.

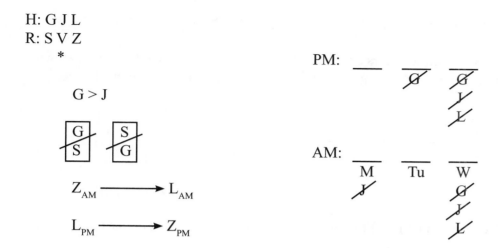

H: G J L
R: S V Z

$G > J$

$Z_{AM} \longrightarrow L_{AM}$

$L_{PM} \longrightarrow Z_{PM}$

The first rule, which states that hotels are not inspected on Wednesday, leads to an interesting set of inferences. First, the three hotels—G, J, and L—must be inspected on Monday and Tuesday, and thus only S, V, and Z are available for inspection on Wednesday. Therefore, exactly two of S, V, and Z are inspected on Wednesday, and G, J, L, and the remainder of S, V, and Z are inspected on Monday and Tuesday.

Because G, J, and L must be inspected on Monday and Tuesday, further inferences can be drawn about the relationship of G and J. Because G must be inspected at some time before J, G cannot be inspected on Tuesday afternoon, and if G is inspected on Tuesday morning, then J must be inspected on Tuesday afternoon.

These relationships are tested repeatedly:

Question #15. The question asks for a pair of buildings that can only be inspected together on Monday. G is a natural choice for analysis since G is so restricted: G cannot be inspected on Wednesday, and if G is inspected on Tuesday, G must be inspected with J. Thus, if G is paired with any other variable besides J, that pairing must occur on Monday. Therefore, any answer choice pairing G and L, S, V, or Z would be correct. Only answer choice (B) makes such a pairing.

Question #16. If G is inspected on Tuesday, then G must be inspected on Tuesday morning and J must be inspected on Tuesday afternoon. Answer choices (C) and (D) can immediately be eliminated.

Question #17. If S is inspected on Monday morning, G cannot be inspected on Monday afternoon, and since G can never be inspected on Tuesday afternoon, we can determine that G must be inspected on Tuesday morning, and the following setup results:

	M	Tu	W
PM	L	J	Z
AM	S	G	V

Overall, this is a tough game.

Advanced Linear Game: Balanced, Identify the Possibilities

The setup below is drawn from the PowerScore LSAT Logic Games Bible.

Notably, either the three bills or the three voters could be chosen as the base. Operationally they will produce no difference. We have chosen to use the three bills as the base and create stacks for Fu, Gianola, and Herstein:

```
H:    __    __    __
G:    __    __    __
F:    __    __    __
      R     S     T
```

The choice of voting for (F) or against (A) will fill each space. Applying the rules creates the following basic diagram:

```
H:    __    __    A      (at lst 1F)
G:    A     __    __     (at lst 1F)
F:    F     A     __
      R     S     T
      (2F,  (1F,  (1F,
      1A)   2A)   2A)
```

The rules provide a considerable amount of specific information: the number of "for" and "against" votes each bill receives; the minimum "for" and "against" votes by Fu, Gianola, and Herstein; and certain votes each voter casts. From the supplied information several inferences can be made. First, since there are two votes for the Recreation bill and one vote against the Recreation bill, and it has already been established that Fu votes for the bill and Gianola votes against the bill, it can be inferred that Herstein votes for the Recreation bill:

```
H:    F     __    A
G:    A     __    __
F:    F     A     __
      R     S     T
```

Furthermore, since only two voting options exist (F or A), dual-options can be placed on the remaining open spaces:

```
H:    F     F/A   A
G:    A     F/A   F/A
F:    F     A     F/A
      R     S     T
```

Of course, further information about some of the dual-options would affect the choices in other dual-options. Regardless, examining the diagram makes it apparent that the voting possibilities are limited. **Game #4 continued on the next page.**

Since there are only four uncertain spaces and even those have restrictions, why not try to show every possibility? Although there are several ways to identify each possibility, the first step we will take is to look at the votes for the school bill. If Gianola votes against the school bill and Herstein votes for the school bill, only one solution exists:

	R	S	T
H:	F	F	A
G:	A	A	F
F:	F	A	A

Possibility #1

In the diagram above, Gianola must vote for the tax bill since each council member votes for at least one bill; since there must be two votes for the tax bill, it can then be inferred that Fu votes for the tax bill.

The other scenario with the school bill switches the votes of Gianola and Herstein:

	R	S	T
H:	F	A	A
G:	A	F	F/A
F:	F	A	F/A

Unfortunately, this information does not completely determine the votes of Fu and Gianola on the tax bill. One must vote for the bill and the other must vote against. Since this produces only two scenarios, show each one:

	R	S	T
H:	F	A	A
G:	A	F	A
F:	F	A	F

Possibility #2

	R	S	T
H:	F	A	A
G:	A	F	F
F:	F	A	A

Possibility #3

Thus, since all the options for the school bill have been explored, it follows that all the options for the entire voting record have been explored. These three solutions comprise the final setup to the game:

	R	S	T
H:	F	F	A
G:	A	A	F
F:	F	A	A

Possibility #1

	R	S	T
H:	F	A	A
G:	A	F	A
F:	F	A	F

Possibility #2

	R	S	T
H:	F	A	A
G:	A	F	F
F:	F	A	A

Possibility #3

October 1999 Game #1: Questions 1-6
Grouping Game: Defined—Moving, Balanced, Numerical Distribution, Identify the Templates

The setup below is drawn from the PowerScore LSAT Logic Games Bible.

Even though the bills appear to have a numerical order, it quickly becomes apparent that they can be paid in any order or configuration. More important are the groups of bills paid on the two days, and the key to the game is the Numerical Distribution of the bills to the days. There are seven bills that must be paid on Wednesday or Thursday, and the first rule establishes that three or four will be paid each day. This leads to two fixed distributions:

	Wednesday	Thursday
Fixed Numerical	3	4
Distributions	4	3

These two fixed distributions suggest Identifying the Templates. We will initially set the game up that way and then discuss the decision to Identify the Possibilities. Let us begin by creating a basic diagram:

1 2 3 4 5 6 7

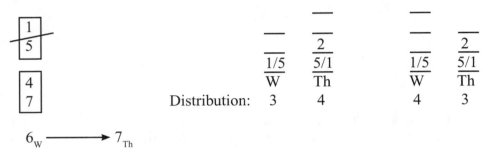

This game also contains a two-value system: all bills must be paid on Wednesday or Thursday. Since bill 1 and bill 5 cannot be paid on the same day, they must be paid on different days. But it is uncertain on which day each is paid, and so a 1/5 dual-option is placed on each day.

The two-value system also affects the last rule. The contrapositive of the last rule is:

$$\cancel{7}_{Th} \longrightarrow \cancel{6}_{W}$$

Of course, if bill 7 is not paid on Thursday it must be paid on Wednesday, and if bill 6 is not paid on Wednesday, it must be paid on Thursday:

$$7_W \longrightarrow 6_{Th}$$

An examination of the final two rules suggests that the number of solutions is limited. Both rules contain bill 7, and especially important is the power of the 4-7 block. When the 4-7 block is applied to the 4-3 distribution, it has only one placement option; when the 4-7 is applied to the 3-4 distribution, it has only two placement options. On the basis of this limitation, a decision should be made to show all the possibilities of those three options. Each appears as follows:

Game #1 continued on the next page.

Possibilities #1 and #2:   Possibilities #3 and #4:   Possibilities #5 and #6:

$$
\begin{array}{cc}
 & \underline{3} \\
\underline{7} & \underline{6} \\
\underline{4} & \underline{2} \\
\underline{1/5} & \underline{5/1} \\
W & Th \\
3 & 4
\end{array}
\qquad
\begin{array}{cc}
 & \underline{7} \\
\underline{3} & \underline{4} \\
\underline{6} & \underline{2} \\
\underline{1/5} & \underline{5/1} \\
W & Th \\
3 & 4
\end{array}
\qquad
\begin{array}{cc}
\underline{3} & \\
\underline{7} & \underline{6} \\
\underline{4} & \underline{2} \\
\underline{1/5} & \underline{5/1} \\
W & Th \\
4 & 3
\end{array}
$$

(4-7 on Wed.)   (4-7 on Thu.)   (4-7 on Wed.)

Each of the three templates includes two possibilities, each dependent on the placement of bill 1 and bill 5. Overall the game has only six solutions. Let us examine each of the three templates in more detail:

> Possibilities #1 and #2: 3-4 Numerical Distribution. When the 4-7 block is placed on Wednesday, no other bills can be paid on Wednesday, and they must all be paid on Thursday. The only remaining uncertainty involves bill 1 and bill 5. Since there are only two options for bill 1 and bill 5, this template contains two solutions.

> Possibilities #3 and #4: 3-4 Numerical Distribution. When the 4-7 block is placed on Thursday, no other bills can be paid on Thursday, and they must all be paid on Wednesday. The only remaining uncertainty involves bill 1 and bill 5. Since there are only two options for bill 1 and bill 5, this template contains two solutions.

> Possibilities #5 and #6: 4-3 Numerical Distribution. The 4-7 block must be placed on Wednesday since there is only one open space on Thursday. When 7 is paid on Wednesday, it can be inferred from the contrapositive of the last rule that bill 6 is paid on Thursday. Since three bills are now paid on Thursday, bill 3 must be paid on Wednesday. The only remaining uncertainty involves bill 1 and bill 5. Because there are only two options for bill 1 and bill 5, this template contains two solutions.

Note that the use of templates to show two possibilities reduces the amount of set up time required. The templates compactly display the uncertainty about bill 1 and bill 5, and there is no need to draw each of the six solutions out individually.

October 1999 Game #2: Questions 7-13
Grouping Game: Defined—Fixed, Unbalanced: Overloaded, Identify the Templates

Hats: N R Y
Jackets: N R Y
Skirts: N R Y
Tie: R

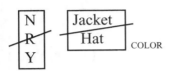

Tie:	R	
Skirt:	R/Y	N
Jacket:	___	___
Hat:	___	___
	1	2

This game is widely regarded as the most difficult game on the October 1999 LSAT. A logical starting point for our analysis is the skirt of mannequin 1. Because mannequin 2's skirt is N, the skirt of mannequin 1 must be R or Y. This inference, when combined with the first two rules, results in a situation where:

1. if the skirt of mannequin 1 is Y, then either the jacket of mannequin 1 is R and the hat of mannequin 1 must be Y or the jacket of mannequin 1 is Y and the hat of mannequin 1 must be R;

2. if the skirt of mannequin 1 is R, then either the jacket and hat of mannequin 1 is some combination of R and Y or of R and N.

Because the options for the jacket and hat of mannequin 1 are restricted according to the color of the skirt of mannequin 1, one approach is to Identify the Templates:

The mannequin 1 skirt is Y:

Tie:	R	
Skirt:	Y	N
Jacket:	R	[N]/[Y]
Hat:	Y	[R]/[N]
	1	2

Tie:	R	
Skirt:	Y	N
Jacket:	Y	[R]/[N]
Hat:	R	[N]/[Y]
	1	2

The jacket and hat on mannequin 2 are locked into a dual-option, which is represented by the two blocks and the slash. For example, if the jacket of mannequin 2 is N, then the hat of mannequin 2 is R.

The mannequin 1 skirt is R:

Tie:	R	
Skirt:	R	N
Jacket:	R	N/Y
Hat:	N/Y	___
	1	2

Tie:	R	
Skirt:	R	N
Jacket:	N/Y	___
Hat:	R	N/Y
	1	2

Game #2 continued on the next page.

This second set of templates is very open, but still quite useful. If you feel that those two templates are insufficient, you can instead show the four basic possibilities when the skirt of Mannequin 1 is R:

Mannequin 1 skirt is R, and the jacket and hat are R and N:

Tie:	R			R	
Skirt:	R	N		R	N
Jacket:	R	N		N	R/Y
Hat:	N	R/Y		R	N
	1	2		1	2

Mannequin 1 skirt is R, and the jacket and hat are R and Y:

Tie:	R			R	
Skirt:	R	N		R	N
Jacket:	R	N/Y		Y	N/R
Hat:	Y	R/N		R	Y/N
	1	2		1	2

October 1999 Game #3: Questions 14-19

Basic Linear Game: Balanced

F G H J K L S

       *

H > K

L > J

F H
or   > K
H F

K L
or   > J
L K

	1	2	3	4	5	6	7
	G̷	J̷	J̷	J̷	F̷	F̷	K̷
	J̷	L̷			H̷	H̷	L̷
	L̷	K̷					F̷
	K̷						H̷

The second, third, fourth, and fifth rules can be combined to create the following chain:

F H		K L
H F		L K

        >   > J

This chain is the key to the game.

An analysis of the most restricted spaces reveals that only F, H, or S can be presented first, and only G, J, or S can be presented seventh.

Question #15 setup:

S	G	F	H	K/L	L/K	J
1	2	3	4	5	6	7

Question #16 setup:

F/H	H/F	G			J/	S/J
1	2	3	4	5	6	7
			J̷	J̷		

This is the easiest game of the October 1999 LSAT.

Basic Linear Game: Unbalanced: Overloaded, Numerical Distribution

F: G H I K
　 *

M: L N O P S
　 *　 *

$\begin{bmatrix} I_F \\ L_M \end{bmatrix}$ $\begin{bmatrix} \overline{} \\ \overline{P_M} \end{bmatrix}$

$K_F \longrightarrow$ 1st F

N/S	K/	/K	G/	/G	P/ /P
					O/ /O
1	2	3	4	5	6
~~K~~	~~G~~	~~G~~	~~K~~	~~K~~	~~K~~
~~G~~	~~H~~	~~O~~		~~I~~	~~I~~
~~H~~	~~I~~	~~P~~		~~L~~	~~L~~
~~I~~	~~L~~				~~G~~
~~L~~	~~O~~				
~~O~~	~~P~~				
~~P~~					

Because K must be the first female to attend a class, we can infer that G, H, and I cannot attend the first class. And, since K cannot attend the first class, the earliest class that K can attend is the second, we can infer that G, H, and I cannot attend the second class. In addition, because I and L form a block, we can infer that L cannot attend the first or second class.

The first, fourth, and fifth rules can be connected to produce a powerful chain sequence:

$$\begin{bmatrix} L_M \\ I_F \end{bmatrix} > G_F > \begin{array}{c} P_M \\ ------ \\ O_M \end{array}$$

Note: O and P could attend the same class.

Without consideration of the other rules of the game, the sequence indicates that O and P cannot be in the first or second class, that I and L cannot be in the fifth or sixth class, and that G cannot be in the sixth class. Consequently, seven of the nine students are eliminated from attending the first class, and therefore only N or S—but not both—can attend the first class. The N/S inference is one of the keys to the game.

In addition, the scenario and rules of the game establish the following unfixed Numerical Distribution:

$$3 - 2 - 1 - 1 - 1 - 1$$
$$P \quad \begin{bmatrix} L \\ I \end{bmatrix} \quad K \quad G$$

When the chain sequence is considered in conjunction with the other rules of the game and the numerical distribution, a number of additional inferences can be made:

　 Either H or O or both must be in the group of three.
　 Either N or S or both must be alone.
　 The group of three must attend either the fifth or sixth class.
　 The group of two must attend either the third or fourth class.
　 The sole attendee at the first class is male.

December 1999 Game #1: Questions 1-5

Grouping Game: Defined—Fixed, Unbalanced: Underfunded

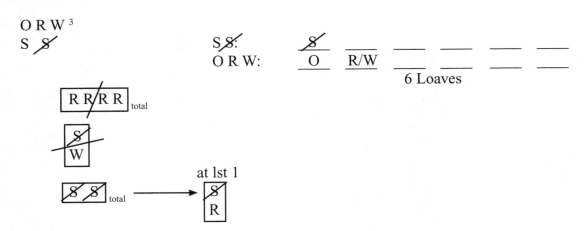

Several of the rules in this game are difficult to represent concisely. In particular, the second and fifth rules reference maximum and minimum total numbers of loaves. We have chosen to show those rules as blocks, with a "total" sub-designation.

The first and fourth rules are easily represented on the diagram. The third rule requires further analysis:

If there are no unsliced wheat loaves, every wheat loave must be sliced:

$$\boxed{\begin{array}{c} \text{S} \\ \text{W} \end{array}}$$

and every unsliced loave must be oatmeal or rye:

$$\boxed{\begin{array}{c} \cancel{\text{S}} \\ \text{O} \end{array}} \quad \text{or} \quad \boxed{\begin{array}{c} \cancel{\text{S}} \\ \text{R} \end{array}}$$

Setup for question #5:

$$\frac{\cancel{\text{S}}}{\text{O}} \quad \frac{\text{S}}{\text{W}} \quad \frac{\text{S}}{\text{W}} \quad \frac{\text{S}}{\text{W}} \quad \frac{\text{S}}{\text{W}} \quad \frac{}{\text{O/R}}$$
6 Loaves

This game seems hard at first because the rules are a bit random; in hindsight the game is very reasonable.

December 1999 Game #2: Questions 6-10
Grouping/Linear Combination Game, Numerical Distribution

F G H L P T [6]

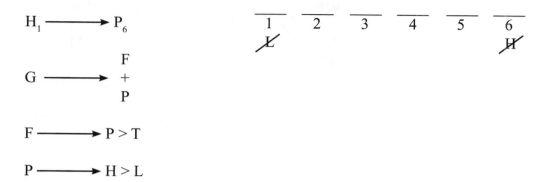

$H_1 \longrightarrow P_6$

$G \longrightarrow \begin{array}{c} F \\ + \\ P \end{array}$

$F \longrightarrow P > T$

$P \longrightarrow H > L$

$$\begin{array}{cccccc} \overline{1} & \overline{2} & \overline{3} & \overline{4} & \overline{5} & \overline{6} \end{array}$$

One of the critical inferences of the game is initiated by the combination of the fourth, fifth, and sixth rules:

$$G \longrightarrow \begin{array}{c} F \\ + \\ P > T \\ + \\ H > L \end{array}$$

The diagram above indicates that if G leaves a message, then every other variable must also leave a message. Thus, since the first two rules create several Unfixed Numerical Distributions, the composition of the people leaving messages under each distribution can be determined:

Unfixed Distribution #1:

1	1	1	1	1	1
F	G	H	L	P	T

All must leave messages, with P > T and H > L. H cannot be first.

Unfixed Distribution #2:

2	1	1	1	1	0
					G

F, P, T, H, and L must be used, with P > T and H > L. H cannot be first.

Unfixed Distribution #3:

3	1	1	1	0	0
				F	G

H, L, P, and T must be used, with H > L

One other inferences: If F leaves a message, then P > T and P cannot leave the sixth message. Via the contrapositive of the third rule, H cannot leave the first message: $F \longrightarrow H_1$. If H does leave the first message, then F cannot leave a message and the 3-1-1-1-0-0 distribution is in effect: $H_1 \longrightarrow$ 3-1-1-1-0-0

R S P ^{3}
F M O T V ^{5}

Wash

Car

$$\underline{R/P} \; \fbox{\underline{\hspace{1cm}} \quad \underline{\hspace{1cm}}} \; \underline{\hspace{1cm}} \; \underline{\hspace{1cm}} \quad R S P$$

$$\underline{V} \quad \underline{\hspace{1cm}} \quad \underline{\hspace{1cm}} \quad \underline{\hspace{1cm}} \quad \underline{\hspace{1cm}} \quad F M O T V$$

1   2   3   4   5

At Lst 1 S

Exactly 1 P

$$\fbox{\underline{\hspace{1cm}}_R \quad M_R}$$

$$\begin{array}{l} O > M > F \\ V > \text{-------------} \\ \qquad\qquad T \end{array}$$

The sequence controls the game and creates four templates:

1.	V	O	M	F	T
2.	V	O	M	T	F
3.	V	O	T	M	F
4.	V	T	O	M	F

These four templates can be linked to the type of wash each car receives:

1.	V	O	M	F	T
	R/P	R	R	S/	/S
2.	V	O	M	T	F
	R/P	R	R	S/	/S
3.	V	O	T	M	F
	P	R	R	R	S
4.	V	T	O	M	F
	P	R	R	R	S

With the templates above the game is relatively easy and certain inferences such as O is always regular, and the second wash is always regular, are made clear.

Note: if you do not wish to make this a multi-stacked game, you can use subscripts for the type of wash each car receives, e.g. M_R.

Basic Linear Game: Balanced

F G H J K M S [7]

F > J

MG

$$\frac{H/}{1} \quad \frac{}{2} \quad \frac{}{3} \quad \frac{S}{4} \quad \frac{}{5} \quad \frac{}{6} \quad \frac{/H}{7}$$

One of the keys to this game is to realize that the MG block is limited in placement, and that when it is before S then M or G must be in 2, and when it is after S then M or G must be in 6. You could create four basic templates to reflect the four positions of the MG block (1-2, 2-3, 5-6, 6-7), but the game appears so simple this is probably unnecessary.

Question #21 setup:

Possibility #1:	H	K	F	S	(MG , J)		
Possibility #2:	F	K	J	S	M	G	H
	1	2	3	4	5	6	7

Most students found this to be the easiest game of the December 1999 LSAT.

June 2000 Game #1: Questions 1-6
Advanced Linear Game: Unbalanced: Overloaded

This Linear game features a 2-2-1-1-1 unfixed numerical distribution. The setup should be quick and straightforward, with the only inferences coming from applying the distribution to the variables.

Boys: F J M P

Girls: N R T

$$\underline{}_{1} \quad \underline{}_{2} \quad \underline{\overset{F}{}}_{3} \quad \underline{}_{4} \quad \underline{}_{5}$$

N/T

T/N

__
J

R

Female / Male

The rules create an Unfixed Numerical Distribution:

7 ——→ 5

2   2   1   1   1

Because J must share a locker, and R cannot share a locker, J must share a locker with N or T. The remainder of N and T must share the other shared locker. These inferences can be applied to the distribution:

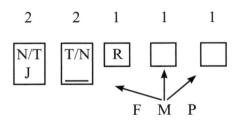

As indicated above, F, M, and P can never share a locker.

Question #1. A List question that should be easily solved given the distribution information above.

Question #6 setup:

M/P	P/M	N/T F	R	T/N J
1	2	3	4	5

June 2000 Game #2: Questions 7-13
Grouping Game: Undefined

On the surface, this game appears to be one of the most difficult of the last several years. The difficulty arises because the store carries ten CDs, but the number of CDs for sale is Undefined. As discussed in the Logic Games Bible, Undefined Grouping games can at times present a severe challenge. Increasing the complexity of the game, four of the rules involve a double conditional. The variables can be listed as follows:

NJ $\quad$ N̶O̶ $\quad$ NP $\quad$ NR $\quad$ NS ^{10}

UJ $\quad$ UO $\quad$ $\boxed{\text{UP}}$ $\quad$ UR $\quad$ US

$\quad\quad$ *

One critical inference involves identifying UO as a random. Because NO is not on sale, and none of the rules involve UO, questions about the CDs that must or cannot be on sale are not likely to involve O. For example, #7 (C), #10 (A), (B), and (C), and #12 (B) each focus on O in a Must be True or Cannot be True question. Because we know nothing about the actions of UO, these answers are likely to be incorrect. A similar line of reasoning can be used to attack question #11. Question #11 asks for what Must be True EXCEPT. Thus, each incorrect answer Must be True, and the correct answer is Not Necessarily True. At first glance, answer choice (A), which addresses UO, is very likely to be correct because we know nothing about the actions of UO and thus almost anything is possible, the opposite of Must be True. Note that, in question #13, the restrictions in the question stem are so severe as to ultimately affect UO.

The diagramming of the rules presents some choices. The second, third, fourth, and fifth rules contain multiple sufficient or necessary conditions. For example, the third rule can be diagrammed as follows:

$$
\begin{array}{ccc}
\text{NJ} & & \text{N̶R̶} \\
+ & \longrightarrow & + \\
\text{UJ} & & \text{U̶R̶}
\end{array}
$$

Some students, however, may find this notation cumbersome. An alternate representation would be to diagram the rule as follows:

$$ \text{J} \longrightarrow \text{R̶} $$

While this representation is easier to digest, because the rules vary between "and" and "or" conditions, some consideration must be given to the impact of those differences. For example, the conditions involving "all," "both," or "neither" could appear with an NU (new and used) designator:

$$ \text{J}_{NU} \longrightarrow \text{R̶}_{NU} $$

Rules involving "either," or contrapositives involving "or" could be diagrammed without designators, thus indicating that the presence of either the new or used type of music would enact the rule.

Ultimately, either representation presents drawbacks: showing each type of music separately is cluttered, whereas using subscripts could be confusing. On the next page we will show both types of diagrams.
Game #2 continued on the next page.

Separate music type representation:

Contrapositives:

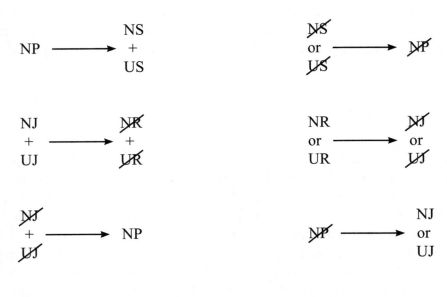

Please note that the second and fourth rules in the game are modified above to reflect the fact that UP must be on sale.

Subscript music type designator representation:

Contrapositives:

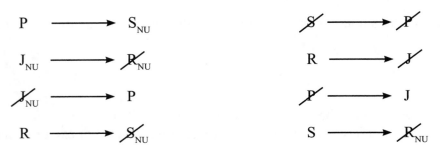

In attacking the game, we choose to use the second set of representations, but if you feel more comfortable with the first set of representations, you can certainly use those instead.

The relationships above lead to several inferences. For example, the first and third rules can be combined:

$$\cancel{J}_{NU} \longrightarrow P \longrightarrow S_{NU}$$

Game #2 continued on the next page.

June 2000 Game #2 continued:

This combination leads to the following inference

$$S\!\!\!/_{NU} \longrightarrow S_{NU}$$

This inference answers question #10, and eliminates answer choices (D) and (E) in question #11.

The last rule and the contrapositive of the second rule can be combined:

$$R \longrightarrow S\!\!\!/_{NU} \longrightarrow P\!\!\!/$$

This combination reduces to:

$$R \longrightarrow P\!\!\!/$$

On some of the questions, a simple application of the contrapositive can be sufficient to answer the question. For example, question #8 can be answered by applying the contrapositive of the second rule.

Largely, solving this game requires a simple application of the rules. However, because there are so many variables and the rules are complex in nature, that application takes time. In addition, the lack of definition makes the game more difficult. Students would have been best served by recognizing that this is an Undefined game with a large number of variables and then pushing this game to last on that basis.

June 2000 Game #3: Questions 14-18
Basic Linear Game: Unbalanced: Underfunded, Identify the Templates

The setup below is drawn from the PowerScore LSAT Logic Games Bible.

The game is Underfunded because three division tours—O, P, and S—must be toured five times (3 into 5). The Underfunded aspect leads to a Numerical Distribution:

> Since S is toured exactly twice and each division is toured at least once, the five tours are distributed among the three divisions in a 2-2-1 partially fixed distribution. The distribution is partially fixed since S is toured twice, but the remaining three tours are assigned to P or O in a 2-1 unfixed distribution:

Partially	2	2	1
Fixed	S	O/P	P/O
Distribution			

> One of the challenges of the game is to keep track of the distribution of O and P.

Initially, most students diagram the game as follows:

O P S ^{3}

Since S is toured twice and the tours are consecutive, the placement options of the SS block are limited to four positions: Monday-Tuesday, Tuesday-Wednesday, Wednesday-Thursday, and Thursday-Friday. These four options split the game in four directions and are the basis for Identifying the Templates:

	M	Tu	W	Th	F
1. SS on Mon-Tue:	S	S	O	O/P	O/P
2. SS on Tue-Wed:	P	S	S	O/P	P/O
3. SS on Wed-Thu:	P	O/P	S	S	O/P
4. SS on Thu-Fri:	P	O/P	O	S	S

With these four templates, the game is easy.

F W T S P [5]

Because the five tasks must be done in order, you must use the tasks as the base of the game, and show the available workers on top. According to the information in the rules, only the following people could complete each of the listed tasks:

I/K	L/O	G/L	H/K/M	H/I/O
F	W	T	S	P

The workers must install the partition in either two or three days, and the rules allow for several different Numerical Distributions:

1-2-2	Unfixed
1-3-1	Fixed
3-1-1	Fixed
3-2	Fixed
4-1	Fixed

A 1-1-3 or a 1-4 fixed distribution is impossible since T and P are done on different days. The 3-2 distribution is possible since the five tasks must be done in *at most three days*. Even though the first rule states that "At least one task is done per day," this allows for a situation wherein the partition completion takes two days and three tasks are done the first day and two tasks are done the second day. As further support, note question #22, which begins, "*If* the installation takes three days..." The first rule about one task per day does rule a distribution such as 3-0-2.

Question #19. The diagram of workers-to-tasks at the top of the page makes this List questions easy to solve. For example, only I or K can do the framing, and therefore either I or K must be on the list. Answer choice (E) contains neither I nor K, and thus answer choice (E) can be eliminated. The same process can be applied to each of the other answer choices.

Question #20. The conditions in the question stem create a 2-1-2 fixed numerical distribution:

2	-	1	-	2
W				P
F		T		S
day 1		day 2		day 3

The question asks you to identify a pair of crew members who could work on both the first and third days. According to our workers-to-tasks diagram, only I, K, L, or O could work on the first day, and only H, K, M, O, and I could work on the third day. Because I, K, and O are common to both days, the correct answer must include two members of that group *and* be a pair who can cover all four tasks. Only K and O meet the criteria.

October 2000 Game #1: Questions 1-6
Grouping/Linear Combination Game

This game bears a striking resemblance to the third game of the December 1994 LSAT. The only difference is that the December 1994 game contained an extra not-block rule.

Reports: G H I K L N O R
Days: M Tu W
Time: AM PM

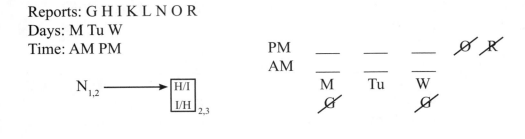

This grouping/linear combination game features eight reports filling six spaces, and thus any time two students are eliminated from the scheduling, the remaining six students must be scheduled. Question #2 is a prime example of the application of this inference. Since neither K nor L is scheduled, G, H, I, N, O, and R must be scheduled. Because O and R cannot give an afternoon report, they must be scheduled for the morning. Only answer choice (D) contains both O and R.

A second application of the above inference is found in question #6. The question stem in #6 indicates that H, K, and L occupy the morning spaces. From the second rule, we can determine that neither O or R can give a report. Thus, the afternoon spaces must be occupied by G, I, and N in some order. The rules indicate that G must give a report on Tuesday afternoon, and therefore N cannot give a report on Monday afternoon. Instead, N must give her report on Wednesday afternoon and I is forced to give his report on Monday afternoon. Answer choice (B) is therefore correct.

Question #4. Given the conditions in the question stem, we can determine that G must give a report on Tuesday. Thus, according to the third rule, N cannot give a report on Monday, and since R, G, and N give reports on different days, N must give a report on Wednesday. Consequently, R must give a report on Monday, in the morning. This information is sufficient to immediately eliminate answer choices (B), (C), and (E). Answer choice (D) can be eliminated since if O were to give a report on Monday, she would have to do so in the afternoon, a violation of the second rule.

Question #5. According to the question stem, K and H give afternoon reports on Tuesday and Wednesday afternoons, respectively. This leaves Monday afternoon as the most restricted space: O and R cannot give reports on Monday afternoon, G cannot give a report on Monday, and N cannot give a report on Monday since K gives a report on Tuesday. Thus, either I or L must give a report on Monday afternoon:

PM	I/L	K	H
AM	___	___	___
	M	Tu	W

Each of the four incorrect answers contains both I and L as students giving morning reports.

October 2000 Game #2: Questions 7-11
Grouping Game: Partially Defined, Numerical Distribution

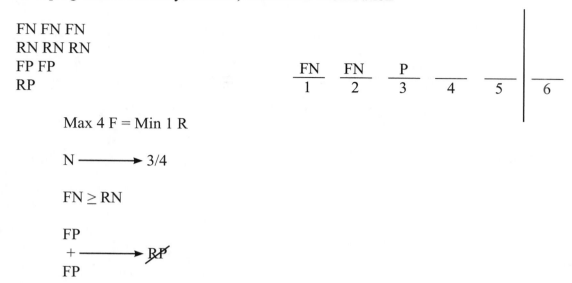

Because the game is partially defined at five or six works selected, the diagram above shows that at least five works must be selected; the bar between the fifth and sixth work indicates that a sixth work can possibly be selected. The combination of the second and third rules create four basic Numerical Distributions for the FN and RN:

FN	$\geq$	RN	
2		1	These four distributions indicate that at least two FN's must be selected. Also, since the maximum number of N's is four, at least one P must be selected.
2		2	
3		1	
3		0	

Other seemingly possible combinations, such as 3-2 or 3-3, are impossible because the maximum number of N is 4. Combinations such as 1-0, 1-1, and 2-0 are impossible because they would cause fewer than five total works to be selected.

The four distributions above have a powerful effect on the questions. For example, on question #8, the distributions show that answer choice (A) could be true and is therefore correct. On question #10, the distributions prove that answer choice (D) is correct. The distribution even has an impact on question #11 as it shows that answer choice (A) is impossible: if no RN's are selected, the maximum number of FN's selected is three, and three FN plus exactly one P equals four total works, one less than the required minimum.

The last rule also bears further analysis. If both FP's are selected, then no RP is selected. But, because at least one R work must be selected, if both FP's are selected then at least one RN is selected.

Overall, the rules in the game are not easy to display conventionally, but if you can focus on the rules involving numbers and thereby create the FN/RN distribution, this game is not difficult.

Basic Linear Game: Balanced

F H L O P R S T [8]

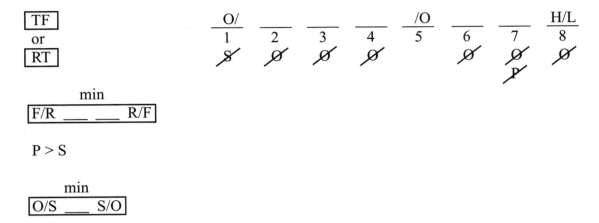

The presence of the words "At least" at the start of the second and sixth rules make this game a bit more difficult than would otherwise be expected. The split-blocks above have the "min" designation in order to indicate that the designated split is the minimum required by the rule. For example, R and F must be separated by at least two spaces, but they could be separated by three or more spaces. Because of this uncertainty in the rules, a large number of the questions are Local.

Question #14 setup:

$$\frac{O}{1} \quad \frac{}{2} \quad \frac{}{3} \quad \frac{}{4} \quad \frac{T}{5} \quad \frac{F}{6} \quad \frac{}{7} \quad \frac{H/L}{8}$$

Because R must be second or third, and P must be performed at some time before S, S cannot be performed second or third.

Question #15 setup:

$$\frac{}{1} \quad \frac{}{2} \quad \frac{R}{3} \quad \frac{T}{4} \quad \frac{O}{5} \quad \frac{F/}{6} \quad \frac{/F}{7} \quad \frac{H/L}{8}$$

Question #17 setup:

$$\frac{O}{1} \quad \frac{}{2} \quad \frac{P}{3} \quad \frac{}{4} \quad \frac{}{5} \quad \frac{S}{6} \quad \frac{}{7} \quad \frac{H/L}{8}$$

The first rule creates either an RT or TF block, and the only remaining place for that block to fit on this diagram is in spaces four and five. Hence, the composition performed fifth must be either F or T.

Advanced Linear Game: Unbalanced: Underfunded, Identify the Templates

G N R ^{3}
H M S ^{3}

| B/B | (crossed out)

1 ⟵———⟶ 7

H = 3

| R | (crossed out)
| H |

pup: <u> G </u> <u> N/R </u> <u>   </u> <u>   </u> <u>   </u> <u> G/R </u> <u> N </u>   G N R
                    Ø̶   N̶   R̶
                                                                   Ø̶

kit: <u> M/S </u> <u>   </u> <u>   </u> <u>   </u> <u>   </u> <u>   </u> <u>   </u>   H M S
       1   2   3   4   5   6   7
      H̶

The second and fourth rules restrict the placement of the H's to four possibilities:

	1	2	3	4	5	6	7
Template #1:			H		H		H
Template #2:		H			H		H
Template #3:		H		H			H
Template #4:		H		H		H	

These four possibilities can be (but do not have to be) used to Identify the Templates

Template #1:

G	N/R	G/N		N/G	G/R	N
M/S	S/M	H	M/S	H	M/S	H
1	2	3	4	5	6	7

Template #2:

G	N	G/R		N/G	G/R	N
M/S	H	M/S	S/M	H	M/S	H
1	2	3	4	5	6	7

Template #3:

G	N	G/R	N/G		G/R	N
M/S	H	M/S	H	M/S	S/M	H
1	2	3	4	5	6	7

Template #4:

G	N	G/R	N/G	R/N	G	N
M/S	H	M/S	H	M/S	H	S/M
1	2	3	4	5	6	7

The only drawback to showing the four templates is that the process can be time-consuming, and overall the questions can still be done without the templates.

December 2000 Game #1: Questions 1-5
Pure Sequencing Game

The setup below is drawn from the PowerScore LSAT Logic Games Bible.

H J L P Q S V [7]

```
                           P
              J  >  Q  > - - - -
         H > - - - - - - - - - - S
              L > - - - - - - - -
                           V
```

```
    H     J/L    ___   ___   ___   ___   P/V
    1      2      3     4     5     6     7
                                          8̸
```

In creating the sequence diagram, the most problematic television program is S. S is less popular than both Q and L, but Q and L are in separate branches. We have solved this problem by placing S at the terminus of the dotted line separator.

As with most Pure Sequencing games, this one is built on top of a linear relationship. H must be the most popular television program and only J or L could be second. Since S cannot be seventh, P or V must be the least popular. With this information we can attack the questions, watching the following two areas:

1. In Pure Sequencing games the test makers always check to see whether you will make unwarranted assumptions about the relationships between the variables.

2. The test makers typically introduce new relationships into the sequence to test your understanding of how the original relationships are affected.

Question #1: Global, Could be true, List question. Apply the rules and inferences in this order: inference that H must be first, fifth rule, second rule, and finally the first, third, and fourth rules can be applied in any order since they are roughly equivalent in form.

Answer choice (A) is incorrect because H must be more popular than J. Answer choice (B) is incorrect because J must be more popular than Q. Answer choice (D) is incorrect because L must be more popular than V. Answer choice (E) is incorrect because S cannot be seventh. Answer choice (C) is correct.

Question #2: Local, Must be true. When examining the linear portion of the setup, take special note of the dual-options. A favorite trick of the test makers is to "take away" one of the variables in a dual-option to see if you recognize that the other variable is then forced into a position. Since either J or L must be second, and according to the question stem J is more popular than L, L cannot be second and J must be second. Answer choice (A) reflects that fact and is correct.

The setup below is drawn from the PowerScore LSAT Logic Games Bible.

Although a maximum of six birds can be in the forest (remember, there are only six birds total), prior to consideration of the rules there could be anywhere from zero to six birds in the forest. This uncertainty increases the difficulty of the game and is an element that must be tracked throughout the game. Of course, since it cannot be determined how many birds are in the forest, there is no "selection group" as in a Defined game:

G H J M S W [6]

Inferences:

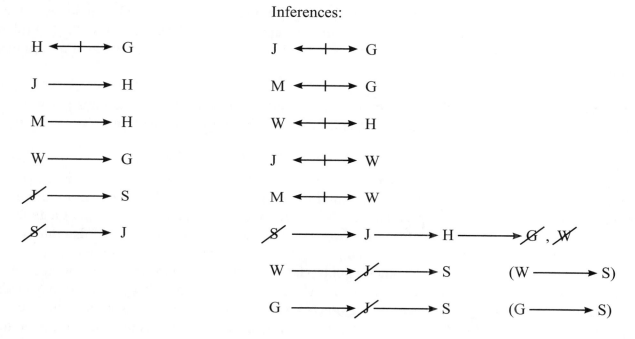

Like many Undefined Grouping games, this one contains a large number of conditional rules. By using basic linkage, we can draw a slew of inferences. Let us examine these in greater detail:

1. J ←—|—→ G. This inference results from linking the first two rules.

2. M ←—|—→ G. This inference results from linking the first two rules.

3. W ←—|—→ H. This inference results from linking the first and third rules.

4. J ←—|—→ W. This inference results from linking the first inference and the third rule. Note how the first inference has been recombined or "recycled" with the original rules.

5. M ←—|—→ W. This inference results from linking the second inference and the third rule. The third rule here refers to the rules as listed in the game.

Game #2 continued on the next page.

December 2000 Game #2 continued:

6. S̶ ⟶ J ⟶ H ⟶ G̶ , W̶. The final rule is a bit unusual and bears further analysis. When J is not in the forest, then S must be in the forest. Via the contrapositive, when S is not in the forest, then J must be in the forest. In each case, the absence of one of the birds forces the other bird to appear in the forest. This type of "omission" rule appears infrequently on LSAT games, but when it does, it tends to cause problems. It is easy to forget that the absence of a variable forces other variables to be present. In this case, when S is not in the forest, then J must be in the forest, and from the second rule, when J is in the forest, it follows that H must be in the forest. Of course, from the first rule and third inference, when H is in the forest, then G cannot be in the forest and W cannot be in the forest.

7. W ⟶ J̶ ⟶ S. From the fourth inference it is known that W and J cannot be in the forest together. Thus, when W is in the forest, then J cannot be in the forest, and from the last rule it follows that S must be in the forest (W ⟶ S). This is another classic example of recycling an inference.

8. G ⟶ J̶ ⟶ S. Similar to the previous inference, when G is in the forest, then J cannot be in the forest, and from the last rule it follows that S must be in the forest (G ⟶ S).

In light of all these inferences, the bigger question becomes, "When do you know you have made all of the inferences?" In this case the application of basic Linkage creates a large number of inferences, and then the recycling of those inferences leads to even more inferences. At some point the time pressure of this section demands that you move on to the questions. Although in our diagram we could continue to make inferences (for example, if H is not in the forest, then J is not in the forest and S must be in the forest), there comes a point when you must ask yourself, "Do I have enough information to effectively attack the questions?" The answer here is undeniably "yes." It may be that you do not discover every inference in the game (as with the first game in this section), but when you feel you have exhausted all the obvious routes of inference-making, it is time to move on to the questions. The challenge in the questions then becomes keeping track of all the information at your disposal.

Ruby: F G H
Saph: J K M
Top: W X Y Z

$\underline{\quad\quad}$ $\underline{\quad\quad}$ $\underline{\quad\quad}$ $\underline{\quad\quad}$ $\underline{\quad\quad}$ $\underline{\quad\quad}$
T   T

2S $\longrightarrow$ 1R $\longrightarrow$ 3T (X, Y, W/Z)

W $\longleftarrow\!\!\!|\!\!\!\longrightarrow$ H

W $\longleftarrow\!\!\!|\!\!\!\longrightarrow$ Z

M $\longrightarrow$ W

<u>Grouping Inferences:</u>

M $\longleftarrow\!\!\!|\!\!\!\longrightarrow$ H

M $\longleftarrow\!\!\!|\!\!\!\longrightarrow$ Z

Either X or Y must be selected.

There are a number of rules that affect the number of stones that can be selected.

- Minimum 2 T (from the first rule)
- Maximum 3 T (W and Z won't go together, making 4 impossible)
- Maximum 3 R (there are only 3 R's)
- Maximum 3 S (there are only 3 S's)
- 2S $\longrightarrow$ 1R $\longrightarrow$ 3T, thus a 2-2-2 distribution is impossible

Using the restrictions above, the following Numerical Distributions can be identified:

Rubies	Sapphires	Topazes
1	3	2
3	1	2
1	2	3
2	1	3
3	0	3
0	3	3

The distribution can be used to answer both question #14 and question #16.

Question #15. If Z is selected, then neither M nor W can be selected. Thus, answer choices (A), (B), and (C), which all contain M, each wrong. Answer choice (D) is incorrect because there would not be enough stones to make six rings. Answer choice (E) can be confirmed by the following hypothetical:
X–Y–Z–F–G–H.

Question #17. Because at least two T's must be selected, and W and Z cannot both be selected, we can deduce that either X or Y or both must be selected. Answer choice (D) is therefore correct.

Question #18. The question stem produces the following scenario: J–M–F/G–W–X–Y.

December 2000 Game #4: Questions 19-23
Basic Linear Game: Unbalanced: Underfunded

This game is reminiscent of the third game on the September 1995 LSAT. That game featured houses in one of three styles—ranch, split-level, and Tudor—on opposite sides of a street

G R Y [3]

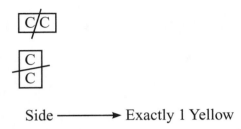

Side ——————→ Exactly 1 Yellow

Because only three colors of lights are available for each store, we can infer that when one color is unavailable there is only a dual-option remaining for that store. This realization is one of the keys to the game. The other key is the restrictive nature of the first two rules. Those rules, diagrammed above using "C" for color, create Not Laws every time the color of the light of a store is determined. For example, from the fourth rule we know that red lights decorate store 4. Consequently, stores 2, 3, and 6 cannot be decorated with red lights. This is the setup for the game:

R	G	Y	G/R	R/G
1	3	5	7	9
G̶	Y̶		X̶	X̶
X̶	R̶			

G/Y	R	G	R/Y	
2	4	6	8	10
R̶		R̶	G̶	
		X̶		

Question #23 is a Suspension question wherein one of the original rules is suspended and replaced by another rule. Because Suspension questions normally require that an entirely new diagram be drawn, this type of question can be time-consuming and should be avoided by slow test takers.

Overall, this is the easiest game of the December 2000 LSAT. Note how this easy game is strategically placed after the difficult third game; Law Services knows that some students will lose so much time in the third game that they will never get to the fourth game. If you are a slow test taker, you can help yourself considerably by knowing the types of games that are easier for you and more difficult for you.

Basic Linear Game: Unbalanced: Underfunded, Identify the Templates

The information in the scenario establishes that five clerks are in a 2-2-2-2-1 Numerical Distribution:

2	2	2	2	1
J	K	L	M	O

J K L M O⁵

L/J	K			K/M				J/L
1	2	3	4	5	6	7	8	9
M̶		K̶	∅̶	∅̶		K̶	K̶	∅̶
K̶		∅̶		L̶			M̶	K̶
∅̶				J̶				M̶

J̶/J̶

M K M
------> O > L
K

L ———▶ 1/9 not both

The "MKM > O > L" sequence is the key to the game. Because M cannot stock aisle 1, the block can be placed no lower than aisle 3. Thus, the MKM block is either in aisles 3-4-5, 4-5-6, or 5-6-7. Consequently, O must stock aisle 6, 7, or 8. Because of the limited placement of the block, only three templates exist:

Template #1:	J/L	K	M	K	M				L/J

Template #2:	J/L	K	L/J	M	K	M	O/	/O	L/J

Template #3:	J	K	L/J	J/L	M	K	M	O	L
	1	2	3	4	5	6	7	8	9

The third template, with the MKM in 5-6-7, is the most restricted, with only two solutions.

June 2001 Game #2: Questions 8-12
Basic Linear Game: Unbalanced: Overloaded, Identify the Possibilities

K L M N O P [6]

The rules reveal the following information about the speaker's specializations:

K/L/M	K/L/M/N	M/N	M/N	N/O/P
1	2	3	4	5

The second rule leads to the powerful inference that since the third and fourth speakers must lecture on M and N, no other speaker can lecture on N and M, leading to the following setup:

K/L	L/K	M/N	N/M	O/P
1	2	3	4	5

This setup can be used as-is, or four basic templates can be created:

	1	2	3	4	5
Template #4:	L	K	N	M	O/P
Template #3:	L	K	M	N	O/P
Template #2:	K	L	N	M	O/P
Template #1:	K	L	M	N	O/P

These four templates contain eight possibilities. With this setup the game is very easy.

Basic Linear Game: Balanced, Identify the Templates

Q R S T V W Y [7]
*

W > S > Y

Template #2:

$\underline{\text{(Q , R > V/T)}}$ $\quad$ $\underline{\text{W}}$ $\quad$ $\underline{\text{(S > Y , T/V)}}$

Template #1:

$\underline{\text{(W > S , R)}}$ $\quad$ $\underline{\text{Y}}$ $\quad$ $\underline{\text{T/V}}$ $\quad$ $\underline{\text{Q}}$ $\quad$ $\underline{\text{V/T}}$

$\quad\quad\quad\quad\quad\quad$ 1 $\quad\quad$ 2 $\quad\quad$ 3 $\quad\quad$ 4 $\quad\quad$ 5 $\quad\quad$ 6 $\quad\quad$ 7

$\quad\quad\quad\quad$ T

R > - - - - - -

$\quad\quad\quad\quad$ V

[T/V]

[V/T]

The rule that establishes that either W or Y arrives fourth triggers the two templates above. Let us take a moment to examine each template in more detail.

Template #1: When Y arrives fourth, both W and S must arrive ahead of Y. The placement of the R, T, V sequence now becomes a problem. If R arrives fifth, then T and V would have to arrive sixth and seventh, a violation of the last rule. Thus, R must arrive before Y. We can now infer that the three trains arriving before Y are W, S, and R, not necessarily in that order. Both T and V must arrive after Y. Because T and V must not arrive consecutively, either T or V must arrive fifth, and the remainder must arrive seventh. Q, the random, must arrive sixth.

Template #2: When W arrives fourth, both S and Y must arrive after W. As in the previous template, the placement of the R, T, V sequence now becomes a problem. R, T, and V cannot all arrive before W, and thus either T or V must arrive after W. Consequently, R and the remainder of remainder of T/V must arrive before W. Q is also forced to arrive before W.

This game serves as another example of the power of rule linkage and interaction. The second and third rules link together in a limiting way, and the fourth and fifth rules link together in a limiting way. When the two sets of rules are combined, their interaction produces a limited number of possibilities, and thus we draw out the two templates. If you have been carefully studying our materials, you should now understand the importance of the Identify the Templates and Identify the Possibilities approach. If you know these techniques and you understand when to apply them, you give yourself a tremendous advantage over other test takers.

Grouping Game: Defined-Moving, Balanced

This game features a two-value system: each doctor must be at either S or R. Thus, if a doctor is not at S, he or she must be at R; if a doctor is not at R, he or she must be at S. The two-value system leads to a number of interesting contrapositives. Ultimately, the game is sufficiently restricted to lead to four templates. First, to help you understand the power of a two-value system, we have diagrammed each of the rules and their contrapositives below.

J K L N O P [6]

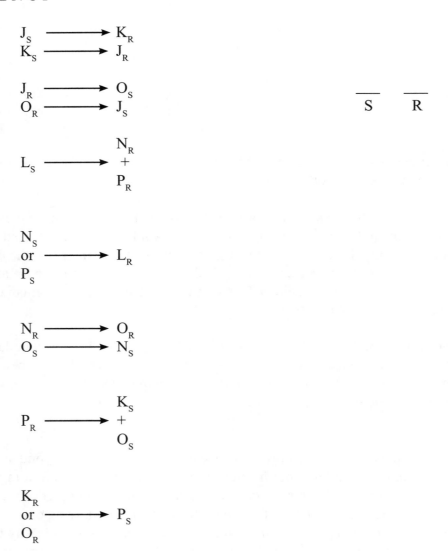

Of course, several of these rules and contrapositives can be combined, such as
$J_R \longrightarrow O_S \longrightarrow N_S \longrightarrow L_R$. With the application of the rules and contrapositives, the game seems only moderately difficult. However, most students fail to apply to two-value system and they will find

Game #4 continued on the next page.

the game rather hard. You can also take the rule relationships a step further, and show four templates containing six total possibilities:

Template #1: O at R

```
              /N
       N/     K
       P      L
       J      O
       S      R
```

Template #2: O at S, K at S, J at R

```
       P/
       K      /P
       N      J
       O      L
       S      R
```

Template #3: O at S, K at R, J at S

```
       P
       J
       N      K
       O      L
       S      R
```

Template #4: O at S, K at R, J at R

```
       P      K
       N      J
       O      L
       S      R
```

Note that the templates reveal one of the challenging inferences of the game: L can never be at S, and thus L must always be at R.

October 2001 Game #1: Questions 1-5

Grouping Game: Defined-Fixed, Unbalanced: Overloaded

This is a Profile Charting game, a variation on a Grouping game. From a Grouping standpoint the game is Defined-Fixed, Unbalanced: Overloaded. The selection pool is subdivided.

In Profile Charting games, one critical step is to examine the profile chart to determine which candidates have identical characteristics. The search for identical pairs must be done because often these identical pairs have natural "opposite" pairs within the game, and consequently powerful hypotheticals can be created. This game contains several such hypotheticals.

F J K L M N P T [8]

Profile Chart:

	E/I	G/R		P/L			
F	E	G					
J	E	R				2E/2I	
K	E	R				2G/2R	
L	E	R					
M	I	G					
N	I	R					
P	I	G					
T	I	G					

From the profile chart, we can determine that J, K, and L are identical, each with the characteristic *ER*. M, P, and T are also identical, each with the characteristic *IG*. Thus, the two groups are perfect opposites, and as long as the rule regarding "either P or L or both are selected" is considered, we can quickly make hypotheticals from the two groups:

Hypotheticals:

J	L	M	P
J	L	M	T
J	L	P	T
K	L	M	P
K	L	M	T
K	L	P	T
J	K	M	P
J	K	P	T

The hypotheticals above solve, or can be used to help solve, question #1 and question #4. The hypotheticals also have the additional benefit of instilling confidence since they contain so much information about the game.

Game #1 continued on the next page.

October 2001 Game #1 continued:

It is also notable that the two remaining variables, F and N, are perfect opposites, and because they are unique in the game, if one appears then the other *must* appear. Both question #3 and question #5 hinge on this inference.

Because F and N are opposites, the remaining two variables that are selected with F and N must also have opposite characteristics. Hence, one variable from the group J, K and L must be selected, and one variable from the group M, P, and T must be selected:

$$\underline{\quad F \quad} \quad \underline{\quad N \quad} \quad \underline{\text{J/K/L}} \quad \underline{\text{M/P/T}}$$

Of course, the P/L rule must still be obeyed.

There are a few simple lessons taught by this game:

1. You must be able to recognize the game type you are facing. Students who recognized this game as a Profile Charting game had a distinct advantage over students who did not recognize the game.

2. When attacking a Profile Charting game you must examine the chart for variables that are identical and variables that are perfect opposites. Use the results of this search to construct hypotheticals.

3. Use the hypotheticals to attack the questions. When you do so, the game becomes incredibly easy.

Grouping Game: Defined-Fixed, Unbalanced: Underfunded, Numerical Distribution

P L S [3]

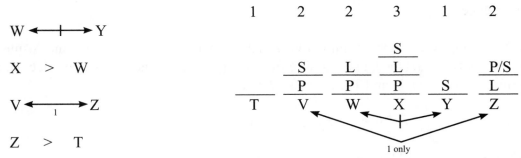

Completing the Numerical Distribution is critical. The following steps create the distribution:

1. Since W has at least two options, and W and Y have no options in common, it follows that W must have exactly two options and Y must have exactly one option.

2. Since X has more options than W, X must have exactly three options.

3. Since T has fewer options than Z, Z must have at least two options. And since V has at least two options and V and Z have only one option in common, it follows that Z cannot have three options. Therefore, Z must have exactly two options. Because of the VZ rule it follows that V cannot have three options and therefore V must have exactly two options.

4. Since Z must have two options, it follows that T must have exactly one options.

5. The above steps create the 1-2-2-3-1-2 Fixed Distribution.

With the distribution, determining most of the options is simple. The only uncertainty in the game is what option T will have, and whether Z will have P or S.

Question #8.

			S		P
	S	L	L		P
	P	P	P	S	L
T	V	W	X	Y	Z

Question #9.

			S		S
	S	L	L		S
P	P	P	P	S	L
T	V	W	X	Y	Z

Game #2 continued on the next page.

Question #10.

```
                        S
           S     L      L              S
    L/P    P     P      P       S      L
    ___   ___   ___    ___     ___    ___
     T     V     W      X       Y      Z
```

Question #11.

```
                        S
           S     L      L              P
     L     P     P      P       S      L
    ___   ___   ___    ___     ___    ___
     T     V     W      X       Y      Z
```

Question #12. The impact of the rule suspension is to create uncertainty over whether X has two or three options. W must still have two options since W and Y have no options in common. If X has two options, then X must have options L and P; if X has three options, then X must of course have options L, P, and S. All other relationships and options remain identical.

Advanced Linear Game: Unbalanced: Underfunded

Q R S T U ^{5} E

K̸ K	G:		R	Q/E ̸X ̸U
		̸X	̸E	̸8

S
--- > T
U

	H:		T/	/T
R Q/S		1	2	3
		̸X	̸E	̸8
				̸U

R Q/S
or both

This game is Underfunded because there are only five variables for six spaces. Since each member of the Kim family can sit in only one seat, it follows that one seat will be empty. In order to more gracefully handle this empty space, you should create an "E" variable to indicate the empty space. This maneuver transforms the game from Unbalanced: Underfunded to Balanced. E is then treated like any other variable.

The following inferences can be drawn:

- The first rule establishes that E cannot sit in seat G2 or H2.

- The second and fourth rules establish that R must sit in row G, and the fifth rule establishes that R must sit in seat G2.

- T must sit in seat H2 or H3. If T sits in H2, then U must sit in H1 and S must sit in G1.

- Seat H3 is occupied by Q, T, or E.

- If E is in seat G3, then seat G1 is Q or S; If E is in seat G1, then seat G2 is Q.

Question #15 setup:

S	R	Q/E
U	T	E/Q
1	2	3

Basic Linear Game: Balanced-Moving, Numerical Distribution

M N O P R S T [7]

	P/	P/	P/			
N	O	R	S	M		T
89	90	91	92	93	94	95

| M O T |Sp

| N R |Sp

| O S |Sp

$$N > \begin{array}{c} P \\ ---- \\ S \end{array} > M$$

The extremely restrictive rule about specialties (Sp) creates a plethora of Not Laws, but also make this game relatively easy. The setup is created by taking the following steps:

1. Since T shares a specialty with M and O, T cannot be hired in years 89, 90, 91, 92, 93, or 94. It follows that T must be hired in 95:

	O	R		M		T
89	90	91	92	93	94	95

2. Due to the sequence, N must be hired in before M; but since N shares a specialty with R, N cannot be hired in years 90, 91, or 92. Therefore, N must be hired in 89:

N	O	R		M		T
89	90	91	92	93	94	95

3. Due to the sequence, S must be hired after N but before M; since S shares a specialty with O, S cannot be hired in years 90 or 91. Therefore, S must be hired in 92:

N	O	R	S	M		T
89	90	91	92	93	94	95

Thus, the only uncertainty in the game is the hiring of P. Since P must be hired after N but before M, P can only be hired in 90, 91, or 92. With so few possibilities, the game is quite easy.

December 2001 Game #1: Questions 1-6
Grouping Game: Undefined

F K O P T W [6]

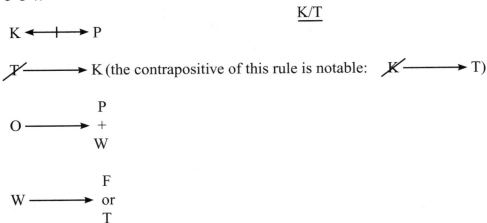

K/T

K ◄——┼——► P

T̸ ——————► K (the contrapositive of this rule is notable: K̸ ——————► T)

O ——————► P
            +
            W

W ——————► F
            or
            T

The first and second rules can be combined:

T̸ ——————► K ——————► P̸

This reduces to:

T̸ ——————► P̸

The contrapositive of this rule leads to the big inference of the game:

P ——————► T

This inference allows the third rule to be restated:

O ——————► P ——————► T
            +
            W

Question #2. Because the second rule indicates that if the stand does not carry T then it must carry K (and by the contrapositive, if the stand does not carry K then it must carry T), the answer must be either K or T. For example, if the fruit stand attempts to carry only F, then by application of the second rule the stand does not carry T and therefore it must carry K. Thus, F cannot be the only kind of fruit that the stand carries. Since the answer must be K or T, and only T appears among the answers, answer choice (D) is correct. An alternate way of looking at the answers is to consider that O, P, and W are all sufficient conditions; that is, their occurrence automatically indicates that other kinds of fruit are carried by the stand. Thus, none of those fruits could be the only fruit carried by the stand.

Question #4. If the stand carries no W, then by the contrapositive of the third rule the stand cannot carry O. The only fruits that can then be carried are F, T, and the choice of K or P. Answer choice (C) is therefore correct.

December 2001 Game #2: Questions 7-13
Advanced Linear Game: Balanced, Identify the Possibilities

F G H I M⁵

L T²

V V S S K⁵

			T			
L/T:	___	___	K	___	___	
City:	___	___	H	___	___	V V S S K
Caller:	I/M	M/I	H	F/G	G/F	F G H I M
	1	2	3	4	5	

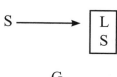

The linkage among the rules ultimately leads to a set of powerful and limiting inferences. The combination of the first and fourth rules establishes that H must call third, and that F and G call fourth and fifth, not necessarily in that order. Because H must call third, H calls from K and is taped. The last rule can now be applied in decisive fashion. If neither M or F calls from S, and H calls from K, then M and F must both call from V. Further, G and I must call from S, and, from the third rule, both calls from S are live. These connections create the following blocks:

V		V		L		L
M		F		S		S
				G		I

The placement options for these blocks is so limited as to make it obvious that we should Identify the Possibilities:

Possibility #1:

	L	T	L	
V	S	K	S	V
M	I	H	G	F
1	2	3	4	5

Possibility #2

L		T	L	
S	V	K	S	V
I	M	H	G	F
1	2	3	4	5

Possibility #3

	L	T		L
V	S	K	V	S
M	I	H	F	G
1	2	3	4	5

Possibility #4:

L		T		L
S	V	K	V	S
I	M	H	F	G
1	2	3	4	5

December 2001 Game #3: Questions 14-18
Advanced Linear Game: Balanced

G H I K L M [6]

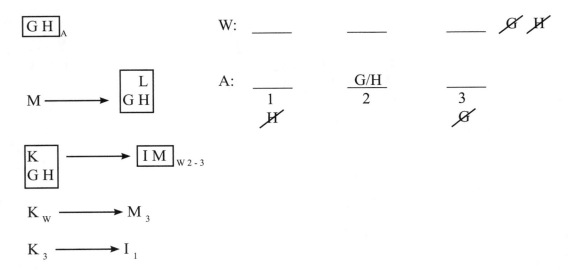

The rules in this game are extremely varied, and this is the most difficult game of the test.

The third rule can only be enacted if K and G sit in row 1. Otherwise, there is no room for the IM block. In fact, the rules are so restrictive that when the K and G rule is enacted there is only one solution to the game:

K	I	M
G	H	L
1	2	3

The second rule also produces a severely limited scenario. When M sits in an aisle seat, M must be in row 1 or 3 in order to accommodate the GH block. However, with the aisle seats filled, K must sit in a window seat. This enacts the fourth rule, which stipulates that when K sits in a window seat, M must sit in row 3:

	L	
G	H	M
1	2	3

Further, the third rule prohibits K from sitting in row 1, and thus K must sit in row 3. Finally, I must sit in row 1:

I	L	K
G	H	M
1	2	3

Game #3 continued on the next page.

At this point, you might be coming to the realization that there are a limited number of solutions to this game. In fact, only seven templates containing fourteen possibilities exist in this game. Although one approach could be to identify each of these templates, there are likely too many templates to be able to show each within the time limits of the game. Normally, we would prefer to draw out four or five templates at most.

With the variety of rules, you should remember that using hypotheticals can be a very effective weapon. If you find yourself unable to identify the inferences in a game, draw out a few solutions to the game; this approach allows you to work with the rules and at the same time increase your knowledge of the game.

The following hypothetical proves answer choice (E) on Question #14 and answer choice (A) on question #15:

I	L	K
G	H	M
1	2	3

Question #16 setup:

M	I/L	L/I
K	G	H
1	2	3

Question #17 setup:

I	L/M	M/L
G	H	K
1	2	3

Question #18 hypothetical:

(I /	L	/ M)
K	G	H
1	2	3

December 2001 Game #4: Questions 19-23

Advanced Linear Game: Balanced, Identify the Templates

F G K L⁴

R S T U⁴

* * *

P:	F	K	G/L	L/G
CP:			/U	U/
	1	2	3	4

```
        min
┌──────────────┐
│ F > ___ > G  │
└──────────────┘
┌───┐
│ L │
│ U │
└───┘
```

The blocks create two basic templates:

P:	F	K	L	G
CP:			U	
	1	2	3	4

P:	F	K	G	L
CP:				U
	1	2	3	4

Question #20 setup:

P:	F	K	L	G
CP:	S/T	T/S	U	R
	1	2	3	4

Question #22. The four different pilot and co-pilot teams that could be assigned to flight 4 are:

L	G	G	G
U	R	S	T

Question #23 setup:

P:	F	K	L	G
CP:	R/T	T/R	U	S/
	1	2	3	4

This game is quite easy, and, like the December 2000 LSAT, serves as another example of the most difficult game appearing third and the easiest game appearing fourth.

RN RS   TN TS   VN VS   WN WS [8]
M M M / F F F F F [8]

North: $\underline{\quad F \quad}$ $\underline{\quad F \quad}$ $\underline{\qquad}$ $\underline{\qquad}$

South: $\underline{\qquad}$ $\underline{\qquad}$ $\underline{\qquad}$ $\underline{\qquad}$
              R   T   V   W

$$VS_M \longrightarrow WN_M$$

Like many games, this game contains a two-value system: each dormitory is assigned either male or female students. Thus, if a dormitory does not have male students, then the dormitory must have female students. As is so often the case, the two-value system can be applied to a conditional rule to create greater insight. Consider the final rule:

$$VS_M \longrightarrow WN_M$$

The contrapositive:

$$\cancel{WN}_M \longrightarrow \cancel{VS}_M$$

Reinterpreted by applying the two-value system:

$$WN_F \longrightarrow VS_F$$

This inference is directly tested in question #3.

Another point of restriction in the game is the males. Because males cannot be assigned to both wings of a dormitory, at most males can be assigned to one wing of a dormitory. At the same time, the rules state that there must be exactly three wings with males. Because there are only four dormitories, the situation is restricted, and the following inferences can be drawn:

1. If a dormitory has female students assigned to both wings, then the males must be assigned to one wing in each of the other three dormitories. For example, if Tuscarora South is assigned females (as in question #5), then males must be assigned to Richards South, Veblen North or South, and Wisteria North or South. In question #5, this inference is sufficient to eliminate answer choices (A), (B), and (E). Answer choice (C) can be eliminated by the contrapositive of the final rule, leaving answer choice (D) as correct.

   Another way to look at this inference is to assert that at only one dormitory can be all-female, and the other three dormitories must each have one male and one female wing.

2. Among any two dormitory pairs, males must *always* be assigned to at least one wing. For example, with Veblen and Wisteria, at least one of the four wings must always be male.

Game #1 continued on the next page.

June 2002 Game #1 continued:

This inference is directly tested in question #2. With Richards and Tuscarora (only south is relevant since the North wings are assigned to females), at least one must always be male, otherwise there will not be a sufficient number of wings available to house the males. Hence, answer choice (B) is correct.

Question #1. The application of the first inference regarding the males creates the following setup:

North:	F	F	F	F/M

South:	M	M	F	M/F
	R	T	V	W

Question #2. As discussed above, with Richards and Tuscarora, at least one must always be male otherwise there will not be a sufficient number of wings available to house the remaining males. Hence, answer choice (B) is correct.

Question #3. The inference that proves answer choice (D) correct is explained above during the discussion of the contrapositive of the final rule.

Question #4. The information in the question stem enacts the last rule, and creates the following setup:

North:	F	F	F	M

South:	F/M	M/F	M	F
	R	T	V	W

Question #5. This question is explained above during the discussion of the restriction of the males.

After a careful consideration of the rules, the only two active rules are the fourth and fifth rules. Obviously, you should pay close attention to these rules as you work through the questions, and indeed, the interaction of these rules creates several powerful inferences that are tested throughout the game. In fact, the inferences are so powerful that only a limited number of templates exist for this game, and one approach would be to show the three basic templates:

> Template #1: Veblen South is male. Two total solutions
> Template #2: Wisteria North is female, Veblen South is female. Four total solutions.
> Template #3: Veblen South is female, Wisteria North is male. Three total solutions.

The choice to show the templates is yours because the game can be done quickly with either approach.

S T U W X Y Z ⁷
R G ²

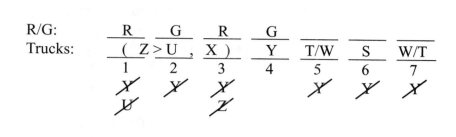

R/R

```
      R          T
- - - - > Y > - - - -
      R          W
```

Z > U

The key to this setup is Y. Because Y must arrive before both T and W, and because S must arrive sixth, the latest that Y can arrive is fourth:

```
              S
            - - - - -
     Y >      T
            - - - - -
              W
```

In addition, because exactly two red trucks arrive before Y, and these red trucks cannot be consecutive, the earliest Y can arrive is fourth:

```
          min
    R ___ R > Y
```

Consequently, because Y can arrive no earlier and no later than fourth, Y must arrive fourth.

Because Y arrives fourth, and S arrives sixth, T and W must arrive fifth and seventh, not necessarily in that order:

R/G:							
Trucks:				Y	T/W	S	W/T
	1	2	3	4	5	6	7

Because exactly two red trucks arrive before Y, and these red trucks cannot be consecutive, they must arrive first and third. The second and fourth trucks must be green in order to comply with the first rule:

R/G:	R	G	R	G			
Trucks:				Y	T/W	S	W/T
	1	2	3	4	5	6	7

Game #2 continued on the next page.

June 2002 Game #2 continued:

The color of the fifth, sixth, and seventh trucks cannot be determined. The remaining three variables, U, X, and Z, must arrive first, second, and third, not necessarily in that order:

R/G:	R	G	R	G			
Trucks:	(Z > U	, X)	Y	T/W	S	W/T	
	1	2	3	4	5	6	7

Question #6. List question. Answer choices (B), (C), (E) can each be eliminated because Y does not arrive fourth (there are also other reasons for eliminating (B), (C) and (E)). Answer choice (D) can be eliminated T arrives ahead of Y, a violation of the second rule. Hence, answer choice (A) is correct.

Question #7. Answer choice (B) is correct because T and S must be consecutive (5-6 or 6-7), and if they are both red then the first rule would be violated.

Question #8. If X arrives third, then according to our diagram Z must arrive first and U must arrive second:

R/G:	R	G	R	G			
Trucks:	Z	U	X	Y	T/W	S	W/T
	1	2	3	4	5	6	7

Hence, U must be green and answer choice (C) is correct.

Question #9. If exactly three trucks are green, then four trucks must be red, and the Separation Principle applies, forcing trucks 1-3-5-7 to be red and trucks 2-4-6 to be green:

R/G:	R	G	R	G	R	G	R
Trucks:	(Z > U	, X)	Y	T/W	S	W/T	
	1	2	3	4	5	6	7

Hence, S must be green and answer choice (A) is correct.

Question #10. In our initial diagram, only Y and S are fixed, and these are the two trucks that meet the criteria. Consequently, answer choice (B) is correct.

Question #11. Because Z must arrive before U, and U must arrive before Y (Z > U > Y), Z and Y cannot arrive consecutively, and answer choice (E) is correct.

Overall, this was the easiest game of the June 2002 LSAT.

Grouping Game: Defined-Fixed, Balanced, Identify the Templates

Grammar: F H
Linguistics: P S
Novels: V W

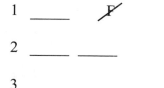

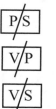

The key to this game is the interaction of the last two rules. Because no two books from the group of V, P, and S can be on the same shelf, each book must occupy a different shelf. And, since there are only three shelves, we can infer that one book from the group of V, P, and S must be on each shelf:

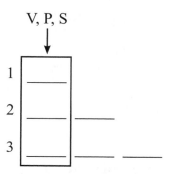

Thus, the first shelf is occupied by either V, P, or S; the second shelf is occupied by either V, P, or S and one other book; the third shelf is occupied by either V, P, or S and two other books.

The interaction of V, P, and S also affects the other three variables, F, H, and W. Using Hurdle the Uncertainty, because the first shelf is occupied, F, H, and W must be on the second and third shelf:

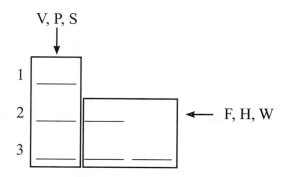

Game #3 continued on the next page.

The only remaining "active" rule is the first rule. Thus, the placement of F must be carefully tracked, and in fact, depending on the placement of W, there are only a few possible templates:

Template #1: F on the second shelf

```
1      P/S

2       V      F

3      S/P     H      W
```

Because F must be on the same shelf as V or W, V must be on the second shelf. P and S form dual-options on the first and third shelves.

Template #2: F on the third shelf, W on the second shelf

```
1      P/S

2      S/P     W

3       V      F      H
```

Because F must be on the same shelf as V or W, V must be on the third shelf. P and S form dual-options on the first and second shelves.

Template #3: F on the third shelf, W on the third shelf

```
1    ┌─────┐

2    │     │   H

3    │     │   F      W
     └─────┘
```

Because F and W are on the same shelf, the first rule is satisfied, and thus V can be assigned to any one of the three shelves.

In total, these three templates contain ten total solutions, and using these templates makes the game considerably easier. However, the game is still time-consuming because there are seven questions.

Game #3 continued on the next page.

Question #12. List question. Answer choice (A) can be eliminated because V and S are on the same shelf, a violation of the third rule. Answer choice (C) can be eliminated because F is not on the same shelf as V or W. Answer choice (D) and (E) can be eliminated because P and S are on the same shelf, a violation of the second rule.

Question #13. From the discussion above, we know that only V, P, or S can be on the first shelf. Hence, no grammar is on the first shelf and answer choice (A) is correct.

Question #14. Template #1 can be used to disprove answer choice (A). Template #2 can be used to disprove answer choice (B). Template #1 can be used to disprove answer choice (A). Template #2 can be used to disprove answer choice (C). Template #2 can be used to disprove answer choice (E). Hence, answer choice (D) is correct.

Question #15. Only template #2 meets the criteria in the question stem, and template #2 proves answer choice (E) is correct. Note that, in template #2, only P and S are uncertain; hence, in a Could be True question you should look for answers that include P or S or both. Only answer choices (A) and (E) include P or S, and looking at those two answers first would reduce the amount of time spent completing the question.

Question #16. From the discussion above, we know that W is always on the second or third shelf. Hence, answer choice (E) is correct.

Question #17. Only template #1 meets the criteria in the question stem, and template #1 proves answer choice (C) is correct. Also, in template #1, only P and S are uncertain; hence, as mentioned above in question #15, in a Could be True question you should look for answers that include P or S or both. Only answer choices (A) and (C) include P or S, and looking at those two answers first would reduce the amount of time spent completing the question.

Question #18. Both template #1 and template #3 meet the criteria in the question stem. An examination of the two templates reveals that the only constant between the two is that W is always on the third shelf. Thus, given that this is a Must be True question, you should immediately look for W on the third shelf. Correspondingly, answer choice (E) is correct. Here are both possibilities with H and P on the same shelf:

1	S/V				1	S		
2	P	H			2	V	F	
3	V/S	F	W		3	P	H	W

Advanced Linear Game: Balanced, Identify the Templates

J K L M O [5]

K/L

M > O J

1	2	3	4	5
Ø	J̸	Ø	J̸	M̸
				L̸

6	7	8	9	10
Ø	J̸	Ø	J̸	M̸
				L̸

The game scenario indicates that laps 1 and 6; 2 and 7; 3 and 8; 4 and 9; and 5 and 10 are all paired, so that a member who swims one lap in the pair automatically swims the other lap in the pair. For example, if a member swims lap 1, he or she also swims lap 6, and if a member swims lap 6, he or she also swims lap 1. Consequently, if a member cannot swim one of the laps in a pair, he or she cannot swim the other lap in the pair. For example, the rules state that J cannot swim lap 9. By deduction, J also cannot swim lap 4.

The pairing of the laps also has an unusual effect on the last rule. The last rule is rather carefully worded to say, "*At least one* of J's laps is immediately after one of O's laps" (italics added). In a regular linear game, a rule like this would normally create an OJ block where J cannot swim lap 1 and O cannot swim lap 5. In this game, however, because laps 5 and 6 are consecutive, J *can* swim lap 1 and O can swim lap 5, as in the following hypothetical:

J	L	M	K	O
1	2	3	4	5

J	L	M	K	O
6	7	8	9	10

In the above hypothetical, J in lap 6 swims immediately after O in lap 5, meeting the specification in the last rule.

In the main diagram, there are several Not Laws worth considering. The last rule produces Not Laws for O on laps 3 and 8. If J cannot swim laps 4 or 9, then O cannot swim laps 3 or 8.

The third rule, M > O, creates two Not Laws because the rule applies to the first lap O swims. Hence, O cannot swim lap 1 (and lap 6) and M cannot swim lap 5 (and lap 10). And, if O cannot swim laps 1 or 6, by applying the last rule we can deduce that J cannot swim laps 2 or 7.

The only remaining Not Law is L on laps 5 and 10. If L swims laps 5 and 10, the OJ block must swim

Game #4 continued on the next page.

laps 2-3 and 7-8. M must then swim laps 1 and 6. The only remaining laps for K to swim are laps 4 and 9, and thus K would swim immediately before L, a violation of the first rule.

A close examination of the game reveals that the placement options of the OJ block are limited. In fact, O and J can only be placed into three separate positions: 2-3 and 7-8; 4-5 and 9-10; 5-6 and 1-10. One approach to the game would be to Identify the Templates:

Template #1: O swims lap 2, J swims lap 3

$$\frac{M}{1} \quad \frac{O}{2} \quad \frac{J}{3} \quad \frac{L}{4} \quad \frac{K}{5}$$

$$\frac{M}{6} \quad \frac{O}{7} \quad \frac{J}{8} \quad \frac{L}{9} \quad \frac{K}{10}$$

Template #2: O swims lap 4, J swims lap 5

$$\frac{(\ M\ ,\ \boxed{K\!\!/\!L}\ )}{1 \qquad 2} \quad \frac{}{3} \quad \frac{O}{4} \quad \frac{J}{5}$$

$$\frac{(\ M\ ,\ \boxed{K\!\!/\!L}\ )}{6 \qquad 7} \quad \frac{}{8} \quad \frac{O}{9} \quad \frac{J}{10}$$

Template #3: O swims lap 5, J swims lap 6

$$\frac{J}{1} \quad \frac{(\ M\ ,\ \boxed{K\!\!/\!L}\ )}{2 \qquad\quad 3 \qquad 4} \quad \frac{O}{5}$$

$$\frac{J}{6} \quad \frac{(\ M\ ,\ \boxed{K\!\!/\!L}\ )}{7 \qquad\quad 8 \qquad 9} \quad \frac{O}{10}$$

Although the above templates make the game quite easy, the original setup to the game can also be used to attack the game effectively.

Question #19. List question. Answer choice (B) can be eliminated because J swims lap 4, a violation of the implications of the second rule. Answer choice (C) can be eliminated because at least one of J's laps is not immediately after one of O's laps. Answer choice (D) can be eliminated because O's first lap is before M's first lap. Answer choice (E) can be eliminated because K's lap is immediately before L's lap. Thus, answer choice (A) is correct.

Game #4 continued on the next page.

Question #20. If J swims lap 8, then, according to template #1 above, all ten lap assignments are determined. Hence, answer choice (A) is correct.

Question #21. If O swims lap 4, then J must swim lap 5 (template #2 above). Accordingly, answer choices (A), (B), (C), and (E) are incorrect. By process of elimination, answer choice (D) must be correct.

Question #22. By applying the Not Laws on our initial diagram, answer choices (A), (C), (D), and (E) can be eliminated. Hence, answer choice (B) is correct.

Question #23. The Not Laws on our initial diagram prove answer choice (B) correct. Note that answer choices (A) and (D) are functionally identical (they reference the same lane pairing), and therefore incorrect.

Question #24. List question. Answer choice (A) can be eliminated because at least one of J's laps is not immediately after one of O's laps. Answer choice (B) can be eliminated because K's lap is immediately before L's lap. Answer choice (D) can be eliminated because J swims lap 9, a violation of the second rule. Answer choice (E) can be eliminated because O's first lap is before M's first lap. Thus, answer choice (C) is correct.

For more information on pure sequencing diagramming, including information on multi-branched verticals and sequencing arrows, see the Logic Games Bible.

Q R S T V W Y Z [8]

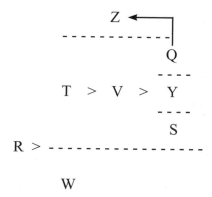

The diagram above governs the order of all eight clowns. From the diagram, we can deduce that either R or Z gets out of the car first. Either R, T, W, or Z get out of the car second, and either Q, Y, S, or W get out of the car last.

Question #1. List question.

   Answer choice (A) is incorrect because T cannot get out of the car first.
   Answer choice (B) is incorrect because Q cannot get out of the car before T or V.
   Answer choice (C) is incorrect because Q cannot get out of the car before Z.
   Answer choice (D) is incorrect because W cannot get out of the car before R.
   Answer choice (E) is the correct answer.

Question #2.

   Answer choice (A) is incorrect because the earliest Y can get out of the car is fourth (this would occur under the sequence R-T-V-Y).
   Answer choice (B) is incorrect because the latest R can get out of the car is second.
   Answer choice (C) is incorrect because the earliest Q can get out of the car is fifth (Q could get out of the car after R, T, V, and Z, in some order).
   Answer choice (D) is the correct answer.
   Answer choice (E) is incorrect because the latest V can get out of the car is fifth (at most, only R, T, W, and Z, in some order, can get out of the car before V).

Game #1 continued on the next page.

Question #3. Because Q gets out of the car at some time after Z, when Z gets out of the car seventh, Q must get out of the car eighth:

$$\underset{1}{\underline{\quad}} \quad \underset{2}{\underline{\quad}} \quad \underset{3}{\underline{\quad}} \quad \underset{4}{\underline{\quad}} \quad \underset{5}{\underline{\quad}} \quad \underset{6}{\underline{\quad}} \quad \underset{7}{\underline{Z}} \quad \underset{8}{\underline{Q}}$$

The remaining clowns are governed by the following sequence:

```
                        Y
        T  >  V  > - - - -
                        S
    R > - - - - - - - - - - - - - - -

        W
```

Consequently, R must be the first clown to get out of the car:

$$\underset{1}{\underline{R}} \quad \underset{2}{\underline{\quad}} \quad \underset{3}{\underline{\quad}} \quad \underset{4}{\underline{\quad}} \quad \underset{5}{\underline{\quad}} \quad \underset{6}{\underline{\quad}} \quad \underset{7}{\underline{Z}} \quad \underset{8}{\underline{Q}}$$

Answer choice (A) is incorrect because R must get out of the car first.
Answer choice (B) is incorrect because T must get out of the car either second or third.
Answer choice (C) is the correct answer.
Answer choice (D) is incorrect because V is either the third or fourth clown to get out of the car.
Answer choice (E) is incorrect because Q is the eighth clown to get out of the car.

Question #4. If T is the fourth clown to get out of the car, then R, W, and Z must each get out of the car ahead of T, and V, Q, Y, and S must all get out of the car after T:

$$\underset{1}{\underline{(\ R>W}} \underset{2}{\underline{,\ Z\ )}} \underset{3}{\underline{\quad}} \quad \underset{4}{\underline{T}} \quad \underset{5}{\underline{(}} \quad \underset{6}{\underline{V>Q}} \underset{7}{\underline{,Y,S}} \underset{8}{\underline{\ )}}$$

Because V must exit ahead of Q, Y, and S, V must exit fifth. Hence, answer choice (D) is correct.

Question #5. If Q is the fifth clown to get out of the car, then S, W, and Y must each get out of the car after Q:

$$\underset{1}{\underline{\quad}} \quad \underset{2}{\underline{\quad}} \quad \underset{3}{\underline{\quad}} \quad \underset{4}{\underline{\quad}} \quad \underset{5}{\underline{Q}} \quad \underset{6}{\underline{(\ S,}} \underset{7}{\underline{W,\ Y}} \underset{8}{\underline{\ )}}$$

Accordingly, W cannot be the fourth clown to get out of the car, and thus answer choice (D) is correct.

Game #1 continued on the next page.

Question #6. If R is the second clown to get out of the car, then Z must be the first clown to get out of the car:

$$\underline{\;Z\;}\;\;\underline{\;R\;}\;\;\underline{\;\;\;}\;\;\underline{\;\;\;}\;\;\underline{\;\;\;}\;\;\underline{\;\;\;}\;\;\underline{\;\;\;}\;\;\underline{\;\;\;}$$
$$\;1\;\;\;\;\;2\;\;\;\;\;3\;\;\;\;\;4\;\;\;\;\;5\;\;\;\;\;6\;\;\;\;\;7\;\;\;\;\;8$$

Accordingly, answer choice (E) is correct.

Question #7. The condition in the question stem creates the following sequence:

$$Z > Q$$
$$- - - - - - -$$
$$T \; > \; V \; > \quad Y$$
$$- - - - - - -$$
$$S$$
$$R \; > -$$

$$W$$

Answer choice (A) is incorrect because R must get out of the car first.
Answer choice (B) is incorrect because, at the latest, T can get out of the car third.
Answer choice (C) is incorrect because, at the earliest, Q can get out of the car fifth.
Answer choice (D) is incorrect because, at the latest, V can get out of the car fourth.
Answer choice (E) is the correct answer.

Overall, this is a great game to encounter first on the LSAT, and the game is tailor-made for the Pure Sequencing Diagramming Guidelines discussed in the Logic Games Bible.

Advanced Linear Game: Balanced

H M P S T W [6]
      * *   *

F F G G L L [6]

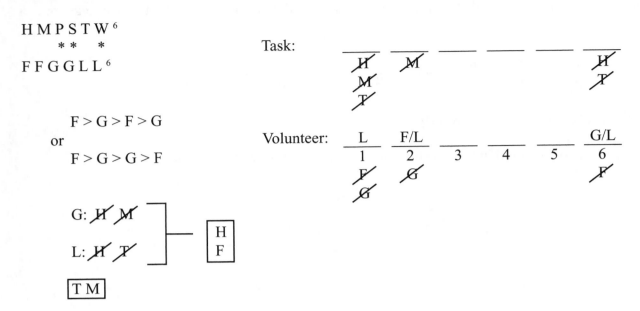

F > G > F > G

or

F > G > G > F

The third and fourth rules combine to produce the inference that F must demonstrate harvesting. And, because F can perform neither first nor last, we can deduce that harvesting is demonstrated neither first nor last.

Because F must perform exactly once prior to G's first performance, G cannot perform first. Thus, since neither F nor G can perform first, L must perform first. Consequently, since L cannot demonstrate threshing, threshing cannot be demonstrated first. And, because threshing cannot be demonstrated first, by applying the last rule we can infer that milling cannot be demonstrated second.

The first rule, which involves F and G, has a controlling effect on the performances of the three volunteers. The rule creates exactly two possible sequences for F and G:

    Sequence 1:   F > G > G > F

    Sequence 2:   F > G > F > G

Because L must perform first, the only wild card in the two sequences above is L's second performance. In the case of Sequence 1, because F cannot perform last, L must perform last, producing just one acceptable ordering of the volunteers:

           L   F   G   G   F   L

In the case of Sequence 2, L's second performance can be second, third, fourth, fifth, or sixth, producing five acceptable orderings of the volunteers:

Game #2 continued on the next page.

L's second performance is second:	L	L	F	G	F	G
L's second performance is third:	L	F	L	G	F	G
L's second performance is fourth:	L	F	G	L	F	G
L's second performance is fifth:	L	F	G	F	L	G
L's second performance is sixth:	L	F	G	F	G	L

Although these six orders limit the possibilities in the game, there are too many combinations of the tasks-to-volunteers to make it worthwhile to Identify the Possibilities or Templates.

Question #8. List question.

    Answer choice (A) is incorrect because F cannot perform first.
    Answer choice (B) is incorrect because F must perform exactly once prior to G's first performance.
    Answer choice (C) is the correct answer.
    Answer choice (D) is incorrect because G cannot demonstrate harvesting.
    Answer choice (E) is incorrect because threshing and milling must be performed consecutively.

Question #9. As mentioned above, because neither G nor L can demonstrate harvesting, F must demonstrate harvesting. Hence, answer choice (A) is correct.

Question #10. If L performs fourth, the application of the first rule (as discussed above) forces the volunteers into the following performance order:

$$\frac{L}{1} \quad \frac{F}{2} \quad \frac{G}{3} \quad \frac{L}{4} \quad \frac{F}{5} \quad \frac{G}{6}$$

Because F must demonstrate harvesting, we can infer that harvesting is demonstrated either second or fifth. Hence, answer choice (B) is correct.

Question #11. The condition in the question stem creates the following block:

P	T	M
G	F	_

Because this block places F after G, by applying the first rule we can infer that F's other performance must come before the block:

H			P	T	M
F	>		G	F	_

Consequently, G's other performance must come after F's first performance, and thus either before or

Game #2 continued on the next page.

after the block. Adding the inference that L performs first creates the following scenario:

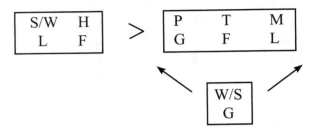

Thus, the only two possible performance orderings of volunteers are:

L-F-G-G-F-L

or

L-F-G-F-L-G

In both scenarios, F will demonstrate harvesting second, and thus answer choice (A) is correct.

Question #12. As mentioned above, because neither F nor G can perform first, L must perform first. Hence, answer choice (D) is correct.

Question #13. The Not Laws created during the setup of this game eliminate answer choices (A), (B), (C), and (D). Thus, by process of elimination, answer choice (E) is proven correct.

Grouping Game: Defined-Fixed, Balanced, Identify the Templates

F G H I W X Y [7]
    *

$$\boxed{\begin{array}{c}H\\Y\end{array}} \quad \cancel{\boxed{\begin{array}{c}F\\G\end{array}}}$$

$$\begin{array}{ccc} & \overline{\quad\quad} & \overline{\quad\quad} \\ \underline{\text{G/}} & \underline{\text{F}} & \underline{\text{/G}} \\ \text{M} & \text{P} & \text{S} \\ \cancel{H} & \cancel{G} & \\ \cancel{Y} & & \end{array}$$

$$X_S \longrightarrow W_P$$

A quick glance at the setup of this game reveals that the placement of the HY block is restricted. Because the HY block can only be hired for positions in the production or sales department, the first step in attacking this game is to examine this restriction by Identifying the Templates:

Template #1: H and Y hired in the production department

$$\begin{array}{ccc} & \underline{\text{Y}} & \underline{\text{I}} \\ & \underline{\text{H}} & \underline{\text{F}} \\ \underline{\text{X}} & \underline{\text{F}} & \underline{\text{W}} \\ \text{M} & \text{P} & \text{S} \end{array}$$

When H and Y are hired for positions in the production department, all remaining applicants must be hired in the management department or the sales department. This directly affects the final rule:

$$X_S \longrightarrow W_P$$

Because there are no remaining positions in the production department for W, we can infer that X cannot be hired in the sales department. This relationship is clearly illustrated by the contrapositive of the last rule:

$$\cancel{W}_P \longrightarrow \cancel{X}_S$$

Hence, because X can be hired in neither the production nor sales departments, X must be hired for a management position. Since all management and production positions are now filled, all remaining applicants must be hired for positions in the sales department. Therefore, when H and Y are hired for positions in the production department, only one solution to the game exists.

Template #2: H and Y hired in the sales department

This template has a greater number of possible outcomes than Template #1. When H and Y are hired in the sales department, there is one remaining position in the management department, two remaining positions in the production department, and one remaining position in the sales department, and these four positions must be filled by G, I, W and X:

Game #3 continued on the next page.

```
              ___
        ___    Y
        F     H
 ___
  M     P     S
```

The second rule affects the placement of all remaining variables:

> If any applicant besides G is hired for the sales position, then G must be hired for the management position, and if any applicant besides G is hired for the management position, then G must be hired for the sales position.

Because there are three other applicants besides G in template #2, when G is hired for the management position, there are three solutions; when G is hired for the sales position, there are also three solutions. The two sub-templates with G hired in management and G hired in sales are shown below.

Let us take a moment to examine the third rule in the context of the template #2. The third rule is the only other "active" rule, but, because of the limited number of remaining spaces, the third rule is actually made superfluous by the controlling action of the second rule. For example, if X is hired for the sales position, then according to the second rule G must be hired for the management position, and then both I and W must be hired for the production positions. This outcome, if X is hired for a sales position then W is hired for a production position, is identical to the outcome produced by the application of the third rule. Therefore, in template #2, the third rule can be ignored, and your attention should be concentrated on applying the second rule when placing the variables.

Template #2A: G is hired for the management position, three solutions

```
                        _____
I, W, X  ──────────▶   |  ___  ___     |
                       |              Y |
                        ‾‾‾   ‾‾‾   ‾‾‾
                        G     F     H
                        M     P     S
```

Template #2B: G is hired for the sales position, three solutions

```
                     _____
                    |  ___        G  |
I, W, X  ──────▶    |  ___        Y  |
                    |___      F   H  |
                       M      P   S
```

Thus, when all of the possibilities from templates #1 and #2 are combined, there are seven solutions to this game.

Game #3 continued on the next page.

Question #14. List question.

Answer choice (A) is incorrect because when X is hired for a sales position then W must be hired for a production position.
Answer choice (B) is because F must be hired for a production position.
Answer choice (C) is incorrect because F and G cannot be hired in the same department.
Answer choice (D) is incorrect because H and Y must be hired in the same department.
Answer choice (E) is the correct answer.

Question #15. From an analysis of the templates above, we know that F, H, I, W, X, and Y can each be hired for a production position. Hence, answer choice (D) is correct.

Question #16. Justify question.

Answer choice (A) is incorrect because templates #2A and #2B both indicate that if F and W are both hired for production positions then there are multiple outcomes.
Answer choice (B) is incorrect because template #2B indicates that there are three possible solutions when G and Y are both hired for sales positions.
Answer choice (C) is the correct answer because I and W can only be both hired for sales positions under template #1, which contains only one solution.
Answer choice (D) is incorrect because the hiring of both I and W for production positions allows for two solutions: one solution under template #2A and another, different solution under template #2B.
Answer choice (E) is incorrect because of the same reasoning cited in answer choice (D).

Question #17. List question. An analysis of template #1 (G-I-W) eliminates answer choice (A). An analysis of template #2A (H-Y-I/W/X) eliminates answer choices (D) and (E). An analysis of template #2B (G-H-Y) eliminates answer choice (C). Thus, by process of elimination, answer choice (B) is proven correct.

Question #18. F and X can only be hired in the same department under template #2, in the production department. Accordingly, H and Y are both hired for positions in the sales department, and answer choice (B) is therefore correct.

Question #19. The condition in the question stem leads to three separate possibilities, one under each template:

Template #1	Template #2A	Template #2B

```
   Template #1              Template #2A              Template #2B

     Y    I                    I    X                    I    G
    ___  ___                  ___  ___                  ___  ___
     H    W                    W    Y                    W    Y
    ___  ___                  ___  ___                  ___  ___
 X   F    G              G    F    H              X    F    H
___ ___  ___            ___  ___  ___            ___  ___  ___
 M   P    S              M    P    S              M    P    S
```

Template #1 proves answer choice (C) correct.

Advanced Linear Game: Balanced, Identify the Templates

N O S T V [5]

N: F L
O: H M
S: G H
T: F G
V: L M

Instrument: ____ ____ ____ ____ ____
Instrument: ____ ____ ____ ____ ____
Piece: ____ N/T ____ ____ ____
          1   2   3   4   5

This can be a challenging game due to the heavy Pattern element of the instruments. In order to effectively attack this game, you must thoroughly analyze the first rule. The rule is very carefully worded to state, "Each piece shares one instrument with the piece performed immediately before it *or* after it (or both)" (italics added). Thus, although a piece can share an instrument with the piece before it *and* with the piece after it, this is not a requirement. Therefore, there can be "breaks" within the performance order where two consecutive pieces do not share an instrument. However, these "breaks" can only appear between certain pieces, namely between the second and third pieces, and between the third and fourth pieces. Let us examine why:

> Because each piece must share an instrument with another piece, we can infer that the first piece must share an instrument with the second piece, and that the fifth piece must share an instrument with the fourth piece.

> The only other consecutive pieces are the second and third pieces, and the third and fourth pieces. A "break" is possible between the second and third pieces: the first and second pieces share an instrument, and then the third piece shares an instrument with the fourth, and the fourth piece shares an instrument with the fifth piece.

> A "break" is also possible between the third and fourth pieces: the first and second pieces share an instrument, the second and third pieces share an instrument, and then the fourth piece shares an instrument with the fifth piece.

The restriction of the first rule, in combination with the second rule, ultimately sparks the decision to Identify the Templates. Because there are only two options for the second performance, and we know from the first rule that the first piece must share an instrument with the second piece, there seems to be an inherent limitation in the pieces that can be performed first and second. There are, in fact, only four possibilities:

> When N is performed second: Because N is performed with fiddle and lute, the first piece must also be performed with fiddle or lute, and thus only T or V can be performed first.

> When T is performed second: Because T is performed with fiddle and guitar, the first piece must also be performed with fiddle or guitar, and thus only N or S can be performed first.

Game #4 continued on the next page.

We can now create the following four templates for the pieces:

Template	1	2	3	4	5
Template #4:	S	T	(N,	O,	V)
Template #3:	N	T	(O,	S,	V)
Template #2:	V	N	(O,	S,	T)
Template #1:	T	N	(O,	S,	V)

Within each template, there also a limited number of possibilities for the pieces performed third, fourth, and fifth; that is, there are not six options in each template as might originally appear to be the case. Let us examine this in more detail, using the first template as an example:

Template #1 features T and N as the first two pieces. Initially, the remaining three pieces—O, S, and V—appear to have six possible orders: O-S-V; O-V-S; S-O-V; S-V-O; V-O-S; and V-S-O. However, due to the restriction of the first rule, only three of these possibilities actually work.

T-N-O-S-V: this possibility fails because V does not share an instrument with S
T-N-O-V-S: this possibility fails because S does not share an instrument with V
T-N-S-O-V: this possibility is a valid solution with no "break"
T-N-S-V-O: this possibility fails because S does not share an instrument with either N or V
T-N-V-O-S: this possibility is a valid solution with no "break"
T-N-V-S-O: this possibility is a valid solution with a "break" between the third and fourth piece

This same type of analysis can be applied to each of the other templates, and each of the other templates also contains three possible solutions:

Template #2. The three solutions are:

V-N-T-O-S
V-N-T-S-O
V-N-O-S-T

Template #3. The three solutions are:

N-T-S-O-V
N-T-S-V-O
N-T-V-O-S

Template #4. The three solutions are:

S-T-N-O-V
S-T-N-V-O
S-T-O-V-N

Game #4 continued on the next page.

October 2002 Game #4 continued:

An examination of the solutions for each template reveals an interesting pattern: the remaining three pieces in each template contain one piece that shares an instrument with each of the other two pieces, but those two other pieces do not share an instrument with each other. For example, in Template #2, S shares an instrument with both O and T, but O and T do not share an instrument with each other. In Template #3 (and Template #1), O shares an instrument with both S and V, but S and V do not share an instrument with each other. In Template #4, V shares an instrument with both N and O, but N and O do not share an instrument with each other. This pattern in part limits the total number of solutions since the two pieces that do not share an instrument cannot be performed fourth and fifth.

In total, the game contains twelve solutions, but it would be quite time-consuming to list each possibility at the start of the game. We recommend that you instead proceed with the four templates, and make note of the basic relationships among the remaining three variables in each template. The templates prove critical to answering several of the questions.

Question #20. List question. An analysis of the templates above reveals that answer choice (D) is correct.

Question #21. At first, this question appears to require more work because you are asked to analyze the instruments played with each piece. However, we know from the second rule that either N or T must be second. N and T have the fiddle in common, so it follows that a fiddle is always used with the second performance. Since each instrument only appears twice among the five pieces (the fiddle is used twice, the guitar is used twice, the harp is used twice, the lute is used twice, and the mandolin is used twice) and the fiddle must be played second, we can infer that the fiddle can never be played in both the third and fourth pieces. Hence, answer choice (A) is correct.

Question #22. The hypothetical V-N-T-S-O can be used to prove answer choice (A) correct.

Question #23. From our discussion of the four templates, we know that only N, S, T, or V could be the first piece performed. Therefore, answer choice (B) is correct.

Question #24. This is a classic final game question—time-consuming and frustrating. If S is performed fifth, then either O or T must apparently be performed fourth. But, T cannot be performed fourth because there is no workable hypothetical with T fourth and S fifth (N must then be performed second, V must be performed first, and then O is left to be performed third, creating a V-N-O-T-S hypothetical that violates the first rule). Hence, O must be performed fourth, and this inference eliminates answer choices (B) and (C). Now that we have established that O will be performed fourth and S will be performed fifth, we can examine the templates to see if any possibilities have been eliminated. Because Template #4 features S as the first performance, we can eliminate Template #4 from consideration. The remaining three templates each feature N as either the first or second performance, and thus we can eliminate answer choice (A). The only remaining answer choices are (D) and (E)—V performed either first or second. Of our three templates (#1, #2, and #3), only Template #2 features V as either the first or second performance, and thus Template #2—which features V as the first performance—proves answer choice (D) correct.

December 2002 Game #1: Questions 1-5
Advanced Linear Game

Red: H M O [3]

Green: P V X [3]
      *

Yellow: T Z [2]
      *

H > O

H/O (boxed, with slash through)

X > V

H > O = X > V (boxed)

Z M (boxed)

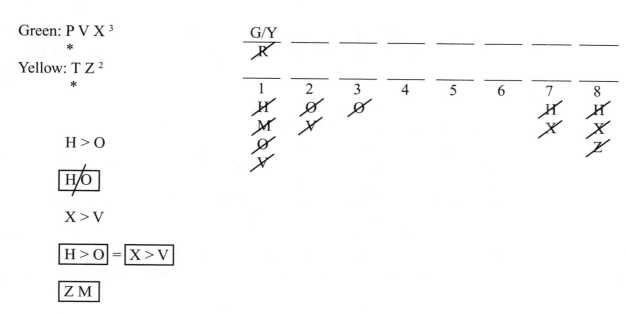

This game is standard, except for the third rule, which is unusual. There are a number of different possible representations of this rule, but we have chosen a diagram that features blocks around the sequences in order to make sure the rule is clear. In our estimation, this representation:

$$\boxed{H > O} = \boxed{X > V}$$

is clearer than:

$$H > O = X > V$$

There are several inferences that can be drawn from this rule, namely:

1. Because the file separation must be equal for both pairs, if X is placed first, V cannot be placed eighth, and if V is placed eighth, then X cannot be placed first. The same relationship applies to H and O (although the last rule already established that H cannot be placed first). Also, V cannot be placed second (since H and O must always be separated by at least one space, therefore if X was first the earliest V could be placed would be third).

2. Because H/O (boxed, slashed), we can infer that X/V (boxed, slashed).

There are also some interesting Not Laws within the diagram:

1. <u>O cannot be placed second.</u> Because H cannot be placed first, and O must be placed in some position after H, we can infer that O cannot be placed second.

Game #1 continued on the next page.

2. <u>O cannot be placed third</u>. The earliest that H can be placed is second. But, because O cannot immediately follow H, we can infer that O cannot be placed third.

3. <u>H cannot be placed seventh</u>. If H is placed seventh, then O must be placed eighth, and that would cause a violation of the rule that states that H cannot immediately precede O.

Question #1. List question.

Answer choice (A) is incorrect because H cannot be placed first.
Answer choice (B) is incorrect because Z must immediately precede M.
Answer choice (C) is incorrect because H cannot immediately precede O.
Answer choice (D) is the correct answer.
Answer choice (E) is incorrect because X and V must be separated by the same number of files as separate H and O.

Question #2. Maximum-Minimum question. This is a perfect question to attack with a hypothetical. Either of the following two hypotheticals of the files only prove answer choice (C) correct:

	1	2	3	4	5	6	7	8
Hypothetical #2:	X	H	V	O	P	T	Z	M
Hypothetical #1:	Z	M	X	P	V	H	T	O

Question #3. The condition in the question stem produces three red-green blocks:

RG		RG		RG

Consequently, a green file can never be placed first. This inference, in combination with the last rule, proves answer choice (A).

Question #4. Maximum-Minimum question. From our initial analysis of the third rule, we know that if X is placed first, then V cannot be placed eighth. However, if X is placed first, perhaps V could be placed seventh. The following hypothetical template proves this is possible:

	1	2	3	4	5	6	7	8
Hypothetical #1:	X	H	(	P,	T,	ZM)	V	O

This hypothetical, one of several possible, proves answer choice (C) correct.

Question #5. Local List question. This question is quite easy. From the Not Laws, we know that H cannot be placed first or seventh, and this information eliminates answer choices (A), (B), and (E). Next, the local condition in the question stem establishes that Z is in the fifth position. From the fourth rule, if Z is in the fifth position, them M must be in the sixth position. This information eliminates answer choice (D), and thus answer choice (C) is correct.

Game #1 continued on the next page.

December 2002 Game #1 continued:

Overall, this is an excellent game to encounter first on the LSAT. As you review the game, closely examine questions #2 and #5 as they both can be effectively attacked by using hypotheticals. Also examine the third rule, and consider how you would diagram such a rule during the test.

M S T ³

min 3 E's

max 2 employees together

R: ____ ____ ____

I: ____ ____ E ~~M~~ ~~S~~

H: ____ ____ ____
　　　 1　 2　 3
　　　　　　~~I~~

At first, this game appears to be fairly standard: nine sessions are being filled, and three employees are available to fill those sessions. The first rule then establishes that each employee can attend only two of the sessions. This rule makes the game appear Underfunded, which is not a concern because we can create three empty spaces to balance out the game. But, the final rule reveals that employees can attend sessions together, and this leaves the number of sessions attended by the employees uncertain. Because we know the employees can attend a maximum of six different sessions or a minimum of four sessions, this game is Partially Defined.

Because the employees can attend a maximum of six different sessions, at least three of the nine sessions will be "empty" for our purposes. These can be designated with "E."

Question #6. Maximum-Minimum question. As mentioned in the discussion above, six is the maximum number of sessions that the Capital employees can attend. Thus, answer choice (D) is correct. Here is one hypothetical that proves the point:

R:	E	S	M
I:	E	T	E
H:	T	M	S
	1	2	3

Question #7. Because M and S can never attend an investing session, and T cannot attend a session on the third day, we were able to deduce in the setup that investing on the third day is empty. Answer choice (E) is impossible and therefore correct.

Question #8. Because T cannot attend a session on the third day, for employees to attend two sessions on the third day then M and S must separately attend the hiring and regulations sessions:

R:	____	____	M/S
I:	____	____	E
H:	____	____	S/M
	1	2	3

This inference allows us to prove that answer choice (C) is correct. For example, if M attends the

Game #2 continued on the next page.

regulations session on day three and S attend the hiring session on day three, then M cannot attend another regulation session and S cannot attend another hiring session. So, if M and S were to attend a session together, they would have to do so at an investing session. But we know from the second rule that M and S cannot attend an investing session. Thus, we can infer that M and S do not attend any session together.

This discussion allows us to make an inference that will be useful later in the game, on question #10: when M and S attend different session topics, i.e. one attends a hiring session and one attends a regulations session (regardless of the day attended), they cannot attend a session together at any point in the game.

Question #9. Like the other Global questions in this game (#6, #7, and #8), this question can be time-consuming. Remember, on many Global questions using hypotheticals is a fast and effective method of attack.

> Answer choice (A) is proven incorrect by the hypothetical provided in question #6.
> Answer choice (B) is the correct answer choice. If the condition in the answer choice is true, then only three sessions would be attended by the employees (two sessions per employee and two employees at each session equals three sessions of two employees each). However, there is no acceptable scenario where this can occur because none of the employees can repeat a session topic.
> Answer choice (C) is proven incorrect by the hypothetical

R:	T	MS	E
I:	E	T	E
H:	MS	E	E
	1	2	3

> Answer choices (D) and (E) are functionally identical, and therefore both are incorrect. M and S are basically interchangeable, and these two answers simply pair S with T, and then M with T. If S can pair with T, then logically M can pair with T. According to the Uniqueness Theory of Answer Choices™, each correct answer choice is identifiably unique, and so any pair of functionally identical answer choices must be incorrect.

Question #10. The condition in the question stem leads to the following basic scenario:

R:	M/S		
I:	T		E
H:	S/M		
	1	2	3

As discussed in question #8, when M and S attend different session topics (as on the first day in this question), they cannot attend a session together at any point in the game. Hence, answer choice (A) is correct.

Game #2 continued on the next page.

December 2002 Game #2 continued:

Question #11. If M and T are the only employees to attend a session on the first day, we can infer that S must attend sessions on both the second day and the third day. And because T cannot attend a session on the third day, T must attend a session on the second day. Thus, M and T attend a session on the first day, S and T attend a session on the second day, and S attends a session on the third day. This information is sufficient to prove answer choice (A) correct.

Advanced Linear Game: Unbalanced, Identify the Templates

S T U W Z⁵ E E

L L L R R⁵ E E

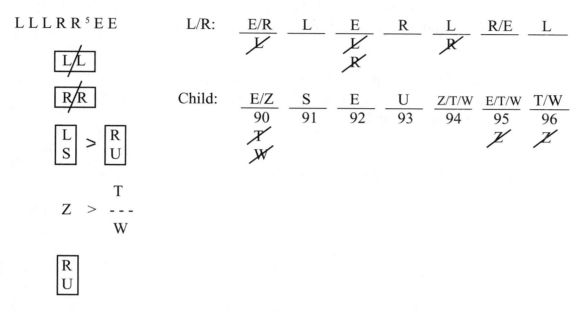

Because there are seven years and only five children, this linear game is Unbalanced. However, this imbalance is easily corrected by creating two empty years, designated by the "E's" above. Since an E in either the L/R row or the child row means that the entire year is empty, we can show the two empty years as:

$$\begin{array}{c} E \\ E \end{array} \quad \text{and} \quad \begin{array}{c} E \\ E \end{array}$$

This game requires a series of related steps to create the complete setup above:

Step 1. The combination of the first rule and the fifth rule allows us to infer that a left-handed child was not born in 1990 or 1992.

Step 2. U, a right-handed child, was born in 1993. Thus, a right-handed chile was not born in 1992 or 1994. Further, from the third rule we can infer that S, a left-handed child, was born in 1990, 1991, or 1992. However, when this inference is combined with step 1, we can infer that S was born in 1991.

Step 3. Since neither a left-handed or a right-handed child can be born in 1992, 1992 must be an empty year. Since a left-handed child cannot be born in 1990, 1990 must be either an empty or a right-handed year.

Step 4. From the first three steps above, we have placed one right-handed child, one left-handed child, and one empty year. Further, 1990 has been established as either an empty or a right-handed year.

Game #3 continued on the next page.

Consequently, two left-handed children must be born in the years 1994, 1995, and 1996. Because of the first rule, we can therefore infer that the two left-handed children are born in 1994 and 1996. From that inference we can deduce that 1995 is the remainder of the right-handed/empty dual-option from 1990. At this point, the entire L/R row is complete, and the only uncertainty is in 1990 and 1995.

Step 5. Due to steps 1 though 4 above, all the rules are "dead" except the fourth rule. The fourth rule is the only remaining active rule, and even then there are limitations, as shown by the dual- and triple-options in the child row of the diagram.

The discussion above reveals the deep restrictions in this game. In fact, there are only two basic templates that exist:

Template #1: Z born in 1990

L/R:	R	L	E	R	L	E	L
Child:	Z	S	E	U	T/W	E	W/T
	90	91	92	93	94	95	96

Template #2: Z born in 1994

L/R:	E	L	E	R	L	R	L
Child:	E	S	E	U	Z	T/W	W/T
	90	91	92	93	94	95	96

Either the original diagram or these two templates can be used to effectively attack this game.

Question #12. List question.

> Answer choice (A) is incorrect because S was born in 1991, not 1990. (A) is also incorrect because no one was born in 1992.
> Answer choice (B) is incorrect because Z was born before both T and W.
> Answer choice (C) is incorrect because U was born in 1993, not 1992.
> Answer choice (D) is incorrect because one of 1990 or 1995 was an empty year.
> Answer choice (E) is the correct answer.

Game #3 continued on the next page.

Question #13. If S was born before Z, then Z must have been born in 1994, as in Template #2:

L/R:	E	L	E	R	L	R	L

Child:	E	S	E	U	Z	T/W	W/T
	90	91	92	93	94	95	96

Consequently, answer choice (D) is proven correct. Also, please note that in this template, the E in the 1990 child row forces a corresponding E in the L/R row, and in turn you can infer that in 1995 a right-handed child was born.

Question #14. Our original diagram proves answer choice (C) correct. If your setup was incomplete, please be aware that you could have used the answer to question #12 to eliminate answer choices (B) and (D).

Question #15. Maximum-Minimum question. The question is specific in requesting the number of different *sequential* orderings, not the number of different orders of children and years. If $W > T$, there are two possible sequential orderings:

Order #1: $Z > S > U > W > T$

Order #2: $S > U > Z > W > T$

Hence, answer choice (B) is correct.

Question #16. The condition in the question stem creates the following scenario, identical to template #1:

L/R:	R	L	E	R	L	E	L

Child:	Z	S	E	U	T/W	E	W/T
	90	91	92	93	94	95	96

Therefore, answer choice (D) is correct.

Again, if you had difficulty creating the scenario above, the solution from question #12 can be used to eliminate answer choices (B) and (E).

Game #3 continued on the next page.

Question #17. If T is right-handed, then T the only year could have been born is 1995. If 1995 is a right-handed year, then 1990 is an empty year, and we can conclude that Z was born in 1994:

L/R:	E	L	E	R	L	R	L
Child:	E	S	E	U	Z	T	W
	90	91	92	93	94	95	96

Thus, answer choice (D) is proven correct.

Question #18. If Z > U, then Z was born in 1990, as in Template #1:

L/R:	R	L	E	R	L	E	L
Child:	Z	S	E	U	T/W	E	W/T
	90	91	92	93	94	95	96

Hence, answer choice (D) is correct.

Once again, if you had difficulty creating the scenario above, the solution from question #12 can be used to eliminate answer choices (A) and (B).

This game is a model example of an Advanced Linear game. Our organized attack features two key pieces: first, we created two "E" placeholders to compensate for the Unbalanced aspect of the game; second, we attacked the rules by linkage, and we kept a close watch on the two not-blocks, especially the LL not-block as the game contained three L's. These two steps reduced the game to a simple exercise in tracking the fourth rule, the only remaining active rule (a quick survey of the questions reveals that every Local question references either T, W, or Z). Students able to recognize the restriction inherent in the fourth rule can then create two templates to attack the game.

J K L M N O P[7]
*   *

                                   <u>Inferences</u>

K $\longleftrightarrow\!\!\!\!|\!\!\!\!\longrightarrow$ O   M $\longleftrightarrow\!\!\!\!|\!\!\!\!\longrightarrow$ K

M $\longleftrightarrow\!\!\!\!|\!\!\!\!\longrightarrow$ N   N $\longleftrightarrow\!\!\!\!|\!\!\!\!\longrightarrow$ K

M $\longrightarrow$ O   M $\longrightarrow$ P

N $\longrightarrow$ O   N $\longrightarrow$ P

O $\longrightarrow$ P   P $\longleftrightarrow\!\!\!\!|\!\!\!\!\longrightarrow$ K

$O_1 \longrightarrow O_2$ M $\longrightarrow O_2$

                                   N $\longrightarrow O_2$

                                   P $\longrightarrow O_2$

At first this game appears to be a fairly standard Grouping game, but the test makers do throw a slight twist into the mix with the last rule that specifies the number of O's selected. Fortunately, this is the only numerical rule, and thus it is easy to remember throughout the game.

Because of the large number of rules, there are also a large number of inferences:

1. M $\longleftrightarrow\!\!\!\!|\!\!\!\!\longrightarrow$ K. This inference is produced by the combination of the first and third rules.

2. M $\longleftrightarrow\!\!\!\!|\!\!\!\!\longrightarrow$ N. This inference is produced by the combination of the first and fourth rules.

3. M $\longrightarrow$ P. This inference is produced by the combination of the third and fifth rules.

4. N $\longrightarrow$ P. This inference is produced by the combination of the fourth and fifth rules.

5. P $\longleftrightarrow\!\!\!\!|\!\!\!\!\longrightarrow$ K. This inference is produced by the combination of the first and sixth rules.

6. M $\longrightarrow O_2$. This inference is produced by the combination of the third and last rules.

7. N $\longrightarrow O_2$. This inference is produced by the combination of the fourth and last rules.

8. P $\longrightarrow O_2$. This inference is produced by the combination of the sixth and last rules.

Game #4 continued on the next page.

December 2002 Game #4 continued:

Two further notes:

 1. In the rule diagrams, the fifth and sixth rules were combined to create the double-arrow representation, which perfectly captures the relationship between O and P.

 2. J and L are both randoms, and in an Undefined Grouping game randoms are very unlikely to have any power at all. Hence, your focus in this game should be almost entirely on K, M, N, O and P.

Question #19. List question.

 Answer choice (A) is incorrect because M and K cannot be selected together; alternately, if M is selected, than at least two O's must be selected.
 Answer choice (B) is incorrect because K and O cannot be selected together.
 Answer choice (C) is the correct answer.
 Answer choice (D) is the incorrect because if one O is selected, than at least two O's must be selected.
 Answer choice (E) is incorrect because M and N cannot be selected together

Question #20. If P is not selected, then O cannot be selected. Via the contrapositive, if O is not selected, then N and M cannot be selected. This information is sufficient to eliminate answer choices (B), (C), (D), and (E). Thus, by process of elimination, answer choice (A) is proven correct.

Question #21. To solve this question, we must first determine which fish species *should* be included; that is, which fish species are necessary to allow other fish species to be chosen. In this game, one fish species stands out as the strongest candidate: O. Because O is a necessary condition for M, N, and P, if O is not selected, then via the contrapositive M, N, and P cannot be selected, a loss of four fish species (O, M, N, P). On the other hand, if O is selected, then O, P, and the choice of M or N can be selected, a total of three selected fish species (O, P, M/N). Clearly, the selection of O has a dramatic positive effect on the maximum number of fish species selected. Hence, if we accept that O should be one of the selected fish species, then from the first rule we can establish that K cannot be selected. Answer choice (A) is therefore correct.

Question #22.

 Answer choice (A) is proven incorrect by the following hypothetical: J J J J.
 Answer choice (B) is proven incorrect by the following hypothetical: L L L L.
 Answer choice (C) is the correct answer. If M is selected, then O must be selected, and if O is selected, then two O's must be selected. Also, if O is selected then P must be selected. So, at a minimum, if M is selected, then at least four fish must be selected.
 Answer choice (D) is proven incorrect by the following hypothetical: O O P.
 Answer choice (E) proven incorrect by the following hypothetical: P O O.

Please note that answer choices (A) and (B) are functionally identical since they both hinge on a random.

Game #4 continued on the next page.

Thus, answer choices (A) and (B) are both incorrect. A similar, but slightly different relationship exists between answer choices (D) and (E). The same hypothetical eliminates each answer choice, so once you determine one answer choice is incorrect, you can eliminate the other answer choice.

Question #23. Maximum-Minimum question. If Barbara selects at least one fish species for her aquarium, the minimum number of fish species she can select is one—she can select either J or L (again, the randoms). Because answer choices (D) and (E) indicate that the minimum number of fish selected is two, both answer choices can be eliminated.

From our discussion in question #21, we know that O is a fish species that should be selected. If O is selected, then we must then also select P. We can also select M or N, but not both. In addition, since J and L are both randoms, we can also select those two species. However, we cannot select K. Thus, the maximum number of fish species Barbara can select is five:

$$O \qquad P \qquad M/N \qquad J \qquad L$$

Thus, answer choice (B) is proven correct.

Overall, this is a very reasonable Games section. The most notable aspect is the high number of False-to-True and Maximum-Minimum questions.

MORE INFORMATION

Additional PowerScore Resources ████████████████

We believe that the *PowerScore LSAT Logic Games Ultimate Setups Guide* is, in combination with *LSAT Logic Games Bible*, the best resource for attacking the Logic Games section of the LSAT.

Because new LSATs appear every several months, and access to accurate and up-to-date information is critical, we have devoted a section of our website to *Ultimate Setups Guide* students. This online resource area offers additional Logic Games information. The *LSAT Ultimate Setups Guide* online area can be accessed at:

www.powerscore.com/lgsetups

If you would like to comment on the *Ultimate Setups Guide*, or make suggestions for additional sections, please send us a message at lgsetups@powerscore.com. We thank you for purchasing this book, and we look forward to hearing from you!

CONTACTING POWERSCORE

Contact Information

PowerScore Full-length LSAT Course Information:
Complete preparation for the LSAT. Classes available nationwide.

Web: www.powerscore.com/lsat/lsat.htm
Request Information: www.powerscore.com/contact.htm

PowerScore Virtual LSAT Course Information:
Complete online preparation for the LSAT. Classes available worldwide.

Web: www.powerscore.com/lsat/virtual.htm
Request Information: www.powerscore.com/contact.htm

PowerScore Weekend LSAT Course Information:
Fast and effective LSAT preparation: 16 hour courses, 99th percentile instructors, and real LSAT questions.

Web: www.powerscore.com/lsat/weekend.htm
Request Information: www.powerscore.com/contact.htm

PowerScore LSAT Tutoring Information:
One-on-one meetings with a PowerScore LSAT expert.

Web: www.powerscore.com/lsat/tutoring.htm
Request Information: www.powerscore.com/contact.htm

PowerScore Law School Admissions Counseling Information:
Personalized application and admission assistance.

Web: www.powerscore.com/lsat/admissions.htm
Request Information: www.powerscore.com/contact.htm

PowerScore International Headquarters:

PowerScore
37V New Orleans Road
Hilton Head Island, SC 29928

Toll-free information number: (800) 545-1750
Facsimile: (843) 785-8203
Website: www.powerscore.com
Email: lsat@powerscore.com